D1551606

Law in the New Republic

*Private Law and the
Public Estate*

BORZOI BOOKS IN LAW AND AMERICAN SOCIETY

Law in the New Republic

Private Law and the Public Estate

George Dargo

ALFRED A. KNOPF NEW YORK

*This book was originally developed as part of an American Bar Association
program on law and humanities with major funding from the National
Endowment for the Humanities and additional support from the Exxon Education
Foundation and Pew Memorial Trust. The ABA established this program to help
foster improved understanding among undergraduates of the role of law in
society through the creation of a series of volumes in law and humanities. The
ABA selected a special advisory committee of scholars, lawyers, and jurists
(Commission on Undergraduate Education in Law and the Humanities) to
identify appropriate topics and select writers. This book is a revised version of
the volume first published by the ABA. However, the writer, and not the
American Bar Association, individual members and committees of the
Commission, the National Endowment for the Humanities, Exxon Education
Foundation, or Pew Memorial Trust, bears sole responsibility for the content,
analysis, and conclusion contained herein.*

THIS IS A BORZOI BOOK
PUBLISHED BY ALFRED A. KNOPF, INC.

First Edition
9 8 7 6 5 4 3 2 1
Copyright © 1983 by Alfred A. Knopf, Inc.

LIBRARY OF CONGRESS CATALOGING IN PUBLICATION DATA

Dargo, George.
    Law in the new republic.

    (Borzoi books in law and American society)
    Bibliography: p.
    Includes index.
    1. Civil law—United States—History. 2. Public
law—United States—History. I. Title. II. Series.
KF361.D37   1982   349.73   82-21244
                              347.3
    ISBN 0-394-33197-4 (Paperbound) 0-394-33581-3 (Casebound)

Manufactured in the United States of America

FOR JESSICA AND STEPHEN

T he life of the law has not been logic: it has been experience. The felt necessities of the time, the prevalent moral and political theories, intuitions of public policy, avowed or unconscious, even the prejudices which judges share with their fellow-men, have had a good deal more to do than the syllogism in determining the rules by which men should be governed. The law embodies the story of a nation's development through many centuries, and it cannot be dealt with as if it contained only the axioms and corollaries of a book of mathematics. In order to know what it is, we must know what it has been, and what it tends to become. We must alternately consult history and existing theories of legislation. But the most difficult labor will be to understand the combination of the two into new products at every stage. The substance of the law at any given time pretty nearly corresponds, so far as it goes, with what is then understood to be convenient; but its form and machinery, and the degree to which it is able to work out desired results, depend very much upon its past.

—Oliver Wendell Holmes, Jr., *The Common Law* (1881)

Preface

This book is about history and law and the relationship between the two. The period it covers encompasses the years when Americans formed their major legal institutions—the Constitution, state governments, the court system, and the organized legal profession. These were years when the law itself went through dramatic changes, and when American attitudes toward the role of law in the development of the nation also changed. Legal historians have referred to this period in a variety of ways: as a "formative era," as a "golden age," and as an "age of discovery" when the law was "Americanized" and "transformed." This book looks at some of those transformations and attempts to explain how and why they happened.

The volume consists of an original essay followed by selected historical documents. The essay provides an explanatory structure, an analytical framework, and general background for understanding the documents. It addresses some new issues and tries to stimulate novel approaches rather than simply retell a familiar story. As for the documents, many are well known while others are more obscure. However, each illustrates an important theme. The main documents are preceded by short introductions describing the specific historical context to which each document refers. The introductory sections also contain several questions for further analysis and discussion. The last part of the book consists of a case study of one particular historical episode. Close examination of these materials offers an opportunity to apply and to test some of the ideas introduced earlier in the book.

The marriage of law and history is not always a happy one. While historians and lawyers both deal with the past, their approaches are radically different. Historians are trained to observe past events, institutions, and ideas through past perspectives while lawyers do so in response to the needs of the present. Historians prefer original, unpublished manuscripts, but lawyers are more comfortable with official documents and published law reports. Historians find answers to questions in a variety of ways and in unlikely locations and often apply different methodologies to documentary as well as nondocumentary sources. Lawyers usually find answers to legal questions within the four walls of a good law library. But practicing lawyers have to investigate facts as well as law. In that respect they, too, become historical detectives and need to utilize all of the skills of the trained historian. Finally, while both disciplines value deep research, the scope of historical inquiry tends toward breadth while the legal researcher seeks to narrow the focus of investigation. In that connection, the historian's definition of relevant evidence and proof is a much broader one than the lawyer's definition.

Thus historians and lawyers bring to the task of history unique skills fostered by different training, discipline, and experience. This book draws upon the techniques and the insights of both. And though it may not satisfy all of the many demands of either history or law, hopefully *Law in the New Republic* displays at least a few of the riches and rewards which interdisciplinary work in legal history can produce.

GEORGE DARGO

Acknowledgments

As with the other volumes in this series, this book began as a project of the American Bar Association's Commission on Undergraduate Education in Law and the Humanities. The four distinguished members of the History Advisory Panel, Professor Stuart Bruchey of Columbia, Stanley N. Katz of Princeton, and John L. Thomas of Brown University, and the Honorable Shirley Abrahamson of the Wisconsin State Supreme Court, contributed important insights and critiques as this book developed from an idea into a manuscript.

A number of other scholars reviewed the work when it was nearer to final form. Their criticisms were often searching and extensive, and I have incorporated many of their suggestions. To Professors Pauline Maier of the Massachusetts Institute of Technology, Robert A. Gross of Amherst College, Stephen E. Patterson of the University of New Brunswick, Paul Finkleman of the University of Texas at Austin, David W. Jordan of Grinnel College, and William E. Leuchtenberg of Columbia University, therefore, I am indeed most grateful.

I also wish to express very special thanks to my good friend, Ms. Paula Snyder, for her invaluable assistance in helping to prepare the manuscript for Alfred A. Knopf, Inc., at a critical time when it was still far from completion.

My family, especially Lois, once again has pitched in by allowing me that extra indulgence which most authors claim and which historians actually deserve.

Contents

I.
Essay

II.
Documents

I. Essay

Introduction

In the half century after the Revolution, America transformed itself from a British colony into an independent nation. From an economic appendage of the British mercantile system, America became a developing commercial power in its own right. The national achievement was impressive. Between 1776 and 1820 America fought two major wars, the war that achieved independence and the War of 1812 that preserved it. American diplomats negotiated the Paris peace settlement in 1783, which made the most of America's military successes in the War of the Revolution, and the Treaty of Ghent in 1815, which minimized American military losses in the second of those wars. In the years of turbulence following the French Revolution and the rise of Napoleon Bonaparte, from 1789 to 1815, America managed to maintain its neutrality for over twenty years. Thereafter it asserted itself as an independent force in the Western Hemisphere. Through all this the nation forged a new relationship among the several states and between the states and the central government with the drafting of the Constitution and its subsequent ratification in 1788. The United States government, a fledgling federal entity, developed viable domestic policies, a two-party system, and an enduring set of political institutions that were the foundation for permanent governmental stability.

During this time, the social and economic fabric of America passed through a rapid sequence of changes. When the shooting started on Lexington Green in the spring of 1775, the American colonies were isolated agricultural settlements clinging to the littoral edge of the vast North American continent. Communication was rudimentary, and intercolonial transportation was very much dependent on coastal travel by sea. Only four cities (Philadelphia, New York, Boston, and Charleston) had populations in excess of 10,000, and these were widely scattered by hundreds of miles. The vast majority of the American people were engaged in agricultural work. There was no national or "continental" economy but a series of fragmented economic zones dependent on the English connection. Such credits in international exchange as the colonists earned resulted from the production of basic raw materials for export to European markets. Total population on the eve of the Revolution was just over 2 million.

By 1820 the nation had grown enormously. Total population was approaching 10 million. Territorial acquisitions from the Treaty of Paris, the Louisiana Purchase, and various treaties and land cessions from Spain put the southern border of the United States on the Gulf of Mexico, and its farthest northwestern reaches on the Pacific. Westward migration was well under way, and the land area east of the Mississippi River was settled, populated, and by 1822, divided into twenty-two separate states and two organized territories. Roads and canals had breached the major geographic land barriers and shortened distances. The first textile factories were already in operation. Steamboats plied the inland rivers. American banks serviced the commercial needs of farmers and townspeople alike. Cities were growing rapidly and were beginning to encounter the social problems of modern urban life—crime, fire, and contagion. In short, by 1820 America had attained not only political independence but considerable economic self-sufficiency and social development.

The conventional wisdom about America's early growth and development holds that the American Revolution, the separation from Great Britain, and the establishment of the federal system of government set loose a spirit of enterprise that was boundless in its ambition, awesome in its energy, and continental in its reach. That spirit was born out of the American passion for freedom, once it was released from the political and legal constraints of English mercantilism. In the 1940s and early 1950s, however, a small band of revisionist historians challenged this view. Sponsored by the Committee on Research in Economic History, and partly funded by the Social Science Research Council, these historians produced a body of work that had a profound impact on American historical writing. The revisionists focused their research on the role of government support in early American development—for reasons that were later explained by two of the leading members of this historical group:

> External conditions influenced the choice of a subject. In the decade or so before the Committee's establishment, the most striking impact upon the study of academic economics had come from government intervention; both the experience of the depression and the broadening scope of state action after World War I had challenged classical assumptions. The Committee therefore focused upon the role of government in the economy as the central subject of its investigations. The outbreak of the war in Europe forced it also to fix its attention on the United States.[1]

The influence of the New Deal on the revisionist historians was clear. The 1930s had witnessed an unprecedented expansion of government intervention in the economy. The "regulatory state" had become a fact of American life. The New Deal transformed the American economic system into a mixed economy in which governmental management moderated the extreme fluctuations of the business cycle. These changes had not come about easily, and the political scars they had caused were still fresh in the 1940s when the work of the revisionist historians began to appear.

The revisionists, although not ideological in a formal sense, were clearly sympathetic to the basic goals and methods of the Roosevelt administration. The results of their work, "a multi-pronged attack on the question of the influence of ... government on the economy of the United States,"[2] was a series of impressive state studies which showed that government, particularly at the state and local levels, had played a crucial role in American economic growth from the very beginning.[3] As one sympathetic writer put it in the introduction to a book on Pennsylvania history: "On the basis of the evidence here presented it seems reasonable to conclude that governmental participation was as great, perhaps greater, in Pennsylvania in 1830 as in 1930, if one takes

---

[1] Oscar Handlin and Mary F. Handlin, *Commonwealth: A Study of the Role of Government in the American Economy: Massachusetts, 1774–1861* (rev. ed. Cambridge, Mass.: 1969; originally published 1947), p. ix.

[2] Ibid.

[3] In addition to the Handlins' *Commonwealth,* these studies included Louis Hartz, *Economic Policy and Democratic Thought: Pennsylvania, 1776–1860* (Cambridge, Mass., 1948); Milton S. Heath, *Constructive Liberalism: The Role of the State in Economic Development in Georgia to 1860* (Cambridge, Mass., 1954); and Carter Goodrich, *Government Promotion of American Canals and Railroads* (New York, 1960).

4 *Law in the New Republic*

into account the scale and range of economic development."[4] Without conscious design, but with considerable effect, these post-New Deal historians established the legitimacy of the New Deal program by demonstrating its source in the American past.

That it was a legitimation in no way diminishes the value of the revisionist contribution to historical knowledge. Awareness of the important supportive role of state and local government in the formative era of America's commercial and industrial growth continues to be a vital corrective to simplistic formulations about "laissez faire," "private initiative," and the "genius of American private enterprise"— clichés that reinforce the mythology of American history, a harmless mythology in itself were it not for its abuse by those with a particular economic and political philosophy.

This essay calls into question some of the conclusions of the revisionist historians. While acknowledging that government enterprise, public subsidies, land distribution policies, state construction of roads and canals, and tax, monetary, and tariff policies contributed substantially to the dramatic growth of the antebellum economy, this work points to the role of American law in sanctioning private decisions, private determinations of value, private standards of liability, and private agreements in American economic development. To that extent it undercuts the stress placed by the revisionists on the role of public law and public authority.

Are these real divergencies of interpretation or merely matters of emphasis and focus? The revisionists analyzed the most visible examples of public policy, principally legislation and regulation. Their orientation was economic. Their research design, as they put it, "focused upon the role of government in the economy as the central subject of . . . investigation." Given such an orientation, it is not surprising that they found that "out of the Revolutionary era emerged a vigorous conception of the state."[5]

In contrast, this essay draws on the materials of legal history. Its focus is common law rather than statutes, courts rather than legislatures, and litigation rather than politics. It is not a general survey of American legal history but an attempt to pose new questions and to offer new perspectives on selected topics and themes. The conclusion it

[4] Benjamin F. Wright, Foreword, in Hartz, *Economic Policy,* p. ix.
[5] Handlin and Handlin, *Commonwealth,* preface to the first edition.

reaches is that while there can be little doubt that government played a critical role in our early economic development, the changes that were taking place in American law indicate that there was a decided movement in this period away from objective, external, and public values toward subjective standards and private decision making. The character of these deep changes in law and the legal system necessarily diminished the "public estate." Despite the acknowledged importance of public authority in fostering development and change, the legal system increasingly emphasized the private resolution of conflict. If the highest social imperative of the eighteenth century had been the pursuit of "public virtue"—willingness of the individual to sacrifice private interest for the good of all—then the decline of the public estate in the nineteenth century represented a basic transformation in American culture and in the American republican experiment itself.[6]

The period covered by this book, therefore, did not simply see the establishment of a new relationship between government and society as suggested by the revisionists. Rather, it saw the emergence of that special reverence for the values, standards, and goals of what has come to be called the "private sector." In that sense the post-Revolutionary period anticipated future historical development even more than has yet been imagined. It was a period in which the conflict between what is public and what is private first appeared, thus creating one of the most enduring tensions in American life.

[6] For a discussion of the concept of public virtue in the eighteenth century, see Gordon S. Wood, *The Creation of the American Republic, 1776-1787* (Chapel Hill, N.C., 1969), pp. 65-70 et passim. (See Document 2.)

1

Law, the Revolution, and the Constitutional Movement

We begin with the Revolution. There are reasons why we should. The Revolution ushered in a period of extraordinary legal activity, which required the participation of a whole new generation of lawyers. At the outset they were not the best known, or the most experienced, or even the ablest lawyers, since many of these sided with the Loyalists and eventually left the country.[1] Nevertheless, the Revolution was very much a "lawyers' revolution." Many Patriot lawyers played important roles at the state and continental levels of government. And the attitudes, values, and institutional changes which emerged in the aftermath of the Revolution, and which continue to this day to animate American public life, were rooted in the legal traditions which were the common experience of that unique generation of American legal professionals.

But if the Revolution was a lawyers' revolution, and if it did cause significant legal change in America, the effect of those changes was uneven. They affected some legal institutions and not others, and some areas of American law more than others. One way of capturing the differentiation is to distinguish between public law and private law. The

---

[1] A recent study of the American Loyalists concludes that while a majority of lawyers were Whig (i.e., Patriots), most of the leaders of the bar, the "giants of the law," remained loyal to the Crown. See Wallace Brown, *The King's Friends: The Composition and Motives of the American Loyalist Claimants* (Providence, R.I., 1965), p. 265. For a discussion of the impact of the Revolution upon the legal profession in one state see Gerard W. Gawalt, *The Promise of Power: The Emergence of the Legal Profession in Massachusetts, 1760–1840* (Westport, Conn., 1979).

7

words "public" and "private" are generally used as opposites. "Private" means belonging to or concerning an individual person, company, or interest. "Public" pertains to the people as a whole—to the nation, state, or community at large. A law is private if it is in the interest of the individual, as distinguished from being for the benefit of the public. Public laws affect the community and all persons within the law's jurisdiction; private law is law that is enforced by individual actions on the basis of common-law doctrines of private rights.

Public law embraces those areas of law that spell out the powers and limitations of government (constitutional and administrative law), those wrongs that the state will prosecute and punish (criminal law), and the methods, processes, and procedures of the legal system itself (procedural law). Lawmaking by the agreement of private parties (contract law), laws that define injuries and wrongs of one party against another in the absence of contractual obligation (tort law), the body of law that establishes the rights, powers, and privileges as well as the duties, obligations, and responsibilities of those owning property (property law), and a host of other subjects (agency, landlord, and tenant law; family law; commercial law) are called private law.[2]

The American Revolution had a deep, abiding, and immediate impact on American public law. In terms of private law, however, its effects were less dramatic and direct. Thus while changes in American law and in the American legal system in the fifty years after the Revolution were profound, those changes cannot be traced directly to the Revolution itself. What is striking, in fact, is the strong continuity of private law in the revolutionary era. Private law was one of those social systems that resisted deep change.[3] To be sure, the law's evolution in the half-century following 1776 was very much the product of social forces that the Revolution had released. But the relationship between law and

[2] Statues of general application are public laws, but private bills—those passed at the petition of individuals—are not. While statutes that have systematized large areas of commercial law, such as the modern Uniform Commercial Code, are part of public law, the body of substantive law thus codified and the continuing interpretation and construction of the UCC is the result of the litigation of private parties and is, to that extent, still part of the private law.

[3] As one noted legal historian has concluded with reference to New England: "The War of Independence had virtually no effect upon the system of private law administered in New England." Richard B. Morris, "Legalism *versus* Revolutionary Doctrine in New England," *The New England Quarterly,* 4 (1931), 195-215, quote at p. 215. See also Stanley N. Katz, "Republicanism and the Law of Inheritance in the American Revolutionary Era," *Michigan Law Review,* 76 (1977), 1-29, which examines the modest impact of the Revolution on inheritance law.

society is complex, and without more evidence than we now have, we cannot conclude that the American Revolution and the changing American legal system were directly connected in a relationship of cause and effect.

This uneven distribution of the reform impulse as between public and private law tells us something about the character of the Revolution and the rather narrow way Americans defined the liberties for which they fought. Their overwhelming desire, after all, was to contain and control political power and to protect private, local rights from governmental interference. The revolutionary generation wanted to circumscribe authority and to define precisely the legitimate functions of government. Consequently, constitutionalism stood at the very center of revolutionary agitation, and constitutional change was the most salient manifestation of the Revolution's effect on American law.[4] Viewing the Revolution retrospectively, the main legal event of the period was the gathering of the Philadelphia Convention of 1787 and the ratification conflict that followed. But for Americans living at the time, the federal structure and the powers of the central government, although important, were questions of far less moment than the constitutional foundations of those governments closest to the people—namely, the states.

On May 10, 1776, almost two months before the Second Continental Congress declared that the North American colonies (except for Canada) were independent from Great Britain, it resolved:

> that it be recommended to the respective assemblies and conventions of the United Colonies, where no governments sufficient to the exigencies of their affairs have been hitherto established, to adopt such government as shall, in the opinion of the representatives of the people, best conduce to the happiness and safety of their constituents in particular, and America in general.[5]

The resolution of May 10 contributed to the resulting agitation for constitutional change, but more likely it was itself a response to that agitation. In either case, from 1776 until nearly the end of the War of Independence most of the American states went through an intensive

---

[4] Gordon S. Wood, *The Creation of the American Republic, 1776–1787* (Chapel Hill, N.C., 1969), chaps. 4, 5, and 6.
[5] Worthington C. Ford (ed.), *Journals of the Continental Congress, 1774–1789* (Washington, D.C., 1904–1937), vol. 4, p. 342.

process of constitution making. Some states even experienced a series of constitutional "revisions" in the course of just a few years, as they experimented with various forms of government and different processes of constitutional adoption.[6]

So central was this preoccupation with constitution making, it even interfered at times with the war effort. For example, in 1777 the New York delegation to the Continental Congress, then meeting in Philadelphia, complained that

> tho' the Enemy is daily expected an astonishing Langour prevails, and the embodying a competent Force to oppose the meditated Invasion, seems to be a distant Object. The Seat of this Disease is not an Indifference to the Cause.... The unhappy Dispute about [the] Constitution is the fatal Rock on which [Pennsylvanians] have split...which threatens them with Destruction. We ardently wish that in our own State the utmost Caution may be used to avoid a like Calamity. Every wise Man here wishes that the Establishment of new Forms of Government had been deferred.[7]

And Robert Morris, chief financial officer of the Confederation, reported to General Horatio Gates that the entire Maryland delegation had gone home in order to participate in the formation of a state constitution. "This seems to be the present business of all America, except the Army," he lamented.[8] As a Virginia delegate concluded regretfully: "Constitutions employ every pen."[9]

But if some members of the Continental Congress understandably saw things from the perspective of the military emergency, many other Americans viewed the constitution-making process much less casually. For them, this was what the Revolution was all about. If the results of independence were to be nothing more than the substitution of one form of oppressive government for another, then the effort was not worth making. Climactic moments in history are infrequent, but this was clearly one of them, and the moment had to be seized. An article in a Philadelphia newspaper printed on July 1, 1776, one day before

---

[6] Willi Paul Adams, *The First American Constitutions: Republican Ideology and the Making of the State Constitutions in the Revolutionary Era* (Chapel Hill, N.C., 1980); Elisha P. Douglass, *Rebels and Democrats: The Struggle for Equal Political Rights and Majority Rule During the American Revolution* (Chicago, 1965).

[7] Philip Livingston, James Duane, and William Duer to Abraham Ten Broeck, April 29, 1777, reprinted in E.C. Burnett (ed.), *Letters of Members of the Continental Congress* (Washington, D.C., 1921–1936), vol. 2, p. 344.

[8] Morris to Gates, October 27, 1776, in ibid., p. 135.

[9] F.L. Lee to Landon Carter, November 9, 1776, in ibid., p. 149.

independence was declared and three days before the Declaration of Independence was adopted, put it best:

> The affair now in view is the most important that ever was before America. In my opinion it is the most important that has been transacted in any nation for some centuries past. If our civil Government is well constructed, and well managed, America bids fair to be the most glorious state that has ever been on earth. We should now at the beginning *lay the foundation right*. . . . The plan of American Government, should, as much as possible, be formed to suit all the varieties of circumstances that people may be in. . . . For we may expect a variety of circumstances in a course of time, and we should be prepared for every condition.[10]

How to "lay the foundation right" was, however, a source of bitter dispute and continuing conflict. The issues were many, some procedural and others substantive. On the procedural side, a much debated question was whether the state legislatures or the people directly, acting through special constitutional conventions, should draft constitutional instruments. The latter was a novel idea, and like most truly revolutionary notions, it was not immediately accepted. The Town Meeting of Concord, Massachusetts, stated the problem with penetrating clarity:

> [If] the same body that forms a Constitution have of consequence a power to alter it [then there is no security for liberty] because a Constitution alterable by the Supreme Legislature is no security at all to the subject against any encroachment of the governing part on any, or on all of their rights and privileges.[11]

If the legislature had the power to draft and adopt a constitution then there would be no true difference between an ordinary statute and the organic or fundamental law. The constitution had to be kept safe from legislative tampering and interference. The most effective way to achieve such a goal was to call into being a special body whose sole purpose was the adoption of a constitution. Once adopted the body would dissolve forever. A constitutional convention was not a continuing body but a special body organized for a special purpose.[12]

[10] *Pennsylvania Packet,* July 1, 1776 (emphasis added); Wood, *Creation of the American Republic,* pp. 127–132 et passim. (See Document 2.)
[11] See Document 1.
[12] While a minority of the states used the convention device either as part of the drafting process or as part of ratification, the federal Constitution of 1787 was both proposed and ratified by the convention method. Thus the process of federal constitution-making was

On substantive issues, such as the structure of government, the powers of the different governmental branches, and the relations between local and central authority, there was deep division between "radicals" who wanted to give maximum authority to the people and "conservatives" who preferred to limit popular sovereignty as much as possible.[13] Included on the radical agenda for constitutional change were the following: (1) the reduction of the role and power of "governors" to that of mere "executives"; (2) provision for legislative impeachment for "executive maladministration"; (3) frequent elections of representatives to the state legislatures; (4) the substitution of residency for property tests in setting voting requirements; (5) separation of the powers of the three functional branches of government to reduce executive influence; and (6) unicameralism in the legislative branch. The most extreme example of radical constitutionalism in action was the Pennsylvania Constitution of 1776, which completely eliminated a single chief executive, established a unicameral legislature, and set up a procedure for periodic revision of the framework of government.[14]

On the other hand, conservatives wanted to maintain property qualifications for voting and for officeholding; they wanted bicameral legislatures so that each branch would serve as a check on the other; and they preferred to increase the power of the executive to counteract the excesses of runaway popular legislatures. While radicals wanted the executives to be chosen by and responsible to the legislatures, conservatives preferred to have the executives elected on their own so that they would have an independent power base that would enable them to withstand legislative "encroachment."[15] Above all, conservatives advocated judicial review of legislative action.

The constitutional convention idea, while innovative and even revolutionary in concept, was also part of the conservative program. Putting the constitution-making process into the hands of the people was one way of keeping it from the legislatures. Conservatives played on

truly innovative, even radical, in its time. Contemporary critics—and liberal historians—focused more upon the conservative substance of the Constitution than the manner of its adoption. See Richard Hofstadter, *The Progressive Historians: Turner, Beard, Parrington* (New York, 1968), chaps. 5–7; Charles A. Beard, *An Economic Interpretation of the Constitution of the United States* (New York, 1913); and Wood, *Creation of the American Republic,* chap. 12.

[13] Adams, *First American Constitutions,* chaps. 6–13, and Douglass, *Rebels and Democrats,* passim.

[14] Ibid., chap. 14.

[15] Wood, *Creation of the American Republic,* chap. 11.

fears of "legislative tyranny." Their program for combating it was to emphasize the distinction between "ordinary law" and "fundamental law"; to support that distinction by giving the people the power to declare the fundamental law in the form of a written constitution; and then to give the courts the function of preserving that distinction through the exercise of the power of judicial review.

The first suggestion that courts should exercise some power of review over legislative enactments came from the conservative camp. New York established a Council of Revision, consisting of the highest executive and judicial officers of the state, whose job it was to review the acts of the legislature.[16] The New York Constitution of 1777—in which the constitutional powers of the governor were unusually broad—was, in fact, a victory for constitutional conservatism. As such, it served as a model for the Founding Fathers in the design of the office of the presidency.[17] The creation at the national level of a powerful chief executive chosen by a special electoral college, rather than by Congress or the state legislatures directly, can be fairly interpreted as a conservative triumph.

On some constitutional issues there was little disagreement between radicals and conservatives. All agreed that a written constitution was preferable to England's unwritten constitution. Americans believed that fixed principles of government were among the immutable "laws of nature."[18] The task of political theorists was to discover those fixed principles, while the task of political activists was to ground those principles in the constitution, the fundamental law of the state. If from an English perspective the strength of the English constitution was its fluidity and its responsiveness to political change, then from an American perspective the strength of American constitutionalism was the detachment of day-to-day politics from those timeless truths about man and government that it wished to preserve for all time.

These ideas were codified in constitutional provisions that defined the constitution as law. The Massachusetts Constitution of 1780 put it this way:

> This form of government shall be enrolled on parchment, and deposited in the Secretary's office, *and be a part of the laws of the land;* and printed

[16] See Document 4.
[17] Compare New York Constitution (1777), Arts. XVII and XVIII, and U.S. Constitution (1787), Art. II (Documents 4 and 6).
[18] George Dargo, "Parties and the Transformation of the Constitutional Idea in Revolutionary Pennsylvania," in *Party and Political Opposition in Revolutionary America,* ed. Patricia U. Bonomi (New York, 1980), p. 110 *et passim.*

copies thereof shall be prefixed to the book containing the laws of this Commonwealth, in all future editions of the said laws [emphasis added].[19]

The notion of written charters having the force and effect of law was not new to Americans. Ever since early colonial times, "charters," "compacts," "orders," "liberties," and "agreements" had been recognized as having legal force.[20] But if it was not a new idea, the Revolution gave it special force and powerful articulation. The use of written constitutions as law was, and remains, a uniquely American contribution to the development of modern government. The French, for example, drafted written constitutions during the French Revolution; but these were little more than frames of government, constitutional blueprints, and statements of political purpose—rather than enforceable legal tools. In America, constitutions had legal authority to which all other law had to conform. As declared by the Massachusetts Constitution:

> [F]ull power and authority are hereby given and granted to the said General Court, from time to time, to make, ordain, and establish, all manner of wholesome and reasonable orders, laws, statutes, and ordinances, directions and instructions, either with penalties or without; *so as the same be not repugnant or contrary to this Constitution* [emphasis added].[21]

Provisions of this kind were significant for two reasons. First, and most important, they made constitutional guarantees of personal liberty enforceable in the courts. In many states these were called bills of rights.[22] Second, they laid the basis for judicial review. While some would argue that "nonrepugnancy" clauses—such as the Massachusetts provision cited above—were not a justification for court review of legislative enactments, particularly in the absence of specific constitutional authorization, it was surely inevitable that high appellate courts would use the written constitution to monitor the decisions of lower courts within their jurisdictions. Thus while the broad reach of John Marshall's decision in *Marbury v. Madison*,[23] outraged many, who labeled it "judicial usurpation," some sort of special constitutional role

[19] Massachusetts Constitution (1780), Chap. VI, Art. XI.
[20] George Dargo, *Roots of the Republic: A New Perspective on Early American Constitutionalism* (New York, 1974), chap. 3.
[21] Massachusetts Constitution (1780), Chap. I, Art. IV.
[22] For example, Virginia Declaration of Rights (1776). (See Document 7.)
[23] See Document 8.

was bound to be played by the courts in a system with a written constitution that was defined as law.[24]

In the end, the idea of a written constitution appealed to radicals and conservatives alike, although in different ways. Radicals liked it because it made legally enforceable such individual rights as religious freedom, security from unlawful arrest, and the right of peaceable assembly and petition. But conservatives also favored the idea because it secured the right to property and was a potential basis for the exercise of the power of judicial review, a power that state as well as federal courts began to exercise with increasing frequency in the decades following the Revolution. Contemporaries perceived the Pennsylvania constitution of 1776, with its unicameral legislature and its plural executive, as the most "radical" of the state constitutions. The New York constitution of 1777, on the other hand, was thought to be a model of "conservatism" because of the great power of the governor's office and the establishment of a special body, the Council of Revision, to review acts of the legislative branch. In fact, almost every state constitution contained some elements of both the "radical" and the "conservative" program. But this should not be surprising since state constitutions were often adopted only after hot political conflict and debate which usually resulted in some kind of compromise and accommodation.

The United States Constitution drafted and ratified by Federalists* (who were seen as "rich and well-born") and opposed by Antifederalists (who had an image of radicalism) contained within it some of the radical program: representation by population in the House, congressional control over military budgets, the power to impeach, the machinery for amendment, specific enumeration of congressional powers, the reservation of powers to the states, and, eventually, the adoption of the federal Bill of Rights showed the impact of radical thought at the federal level. But conservatives could also claim victories: a bicameral Congress, a powerful chief executive, an independent federal judiciary, the equality of the House and Senate, and a prohibition on state legislative impairment of private contractual obligations.

---

[24] For a discussion of judicial review and the intent of the framers, see Raoul Berger, *Congress v. The Supreme Court* (Cambridge, Mass., 1969), chap. 7.

* The term "federalist" was used in the 1780s to denote strong nationalistic proclivities while the term "antifederalist" referred to that political persuasion which would preserve the sovereignty of the states. These terms should not be confused with the Federalist Party and the Jeffersonian opposition which grew out of the policies of the Washington administration in the early 1790s.

However, there was, also, in the federal Constitution an overriding concept on which both radicals and conservatives could agree, each for their own reasons. This was the supremacy clause, which can be thought of as the single most important provision of that great document:

> This Constitution, and the laws of the United States which shall be made in pursuance thereof, and all treaties made, or which shall be made, under the authority of the United States, shall be the *supreme law of the land:* And the Judges in every State shall be bound thereby, *anything in the Constitution or laws of any State to the contrary notwithstanding* [emphasis added].[25]

The supremacy clause was principally designed to give effect to the nationalism of men such as John Jay, Alexander Hamilton, Gouverneur Morris, and George Washington: to bind the states into an organic nation under one supreme law that would be applied by national (or "federal") courts. But in the context of the whole constitutional movement, state as well as federal, the supremacy clause has independent and additional significance. It is the element that most distinguished the Constitution of the United States from the Articles of Confederation adopted in 1781. In giving the Constitution the force of law, the framers created an instrument of government comparable to the state constitutions. This was no mere "league of friendship"[26] among the several states but a true government of awesome potentiality. In that respect its opponents, who feared the enhanced power of the central government, were right to clamor for limitations on the national authority—a clamor that led to the adoption of the federal Bill of Rights.[27] The supremacy clause made the guarantees codified in the Bill of Rights legally enforceable limitations first on Congress and later on government in general.

For all of its economy of statement, therefore, the United States Constitution is extraordinary in its scope. It bound the states as well as the national government into a union of law, and it made the government of the United States truly a "government of laws and not of men."

---

[25] U.S. Constitution (1787), Art. VI.
[26] See Document 5.
[27] Alphens T. Mason, *The States Rights Debate: Antifederalism and the Constitution* (Englewood Cliffs, N.J., 1964), pp. 1–7.

2

The Privatization of Public Law

The revolutionary generation's extraordinary preoccupation with the process of constitution making is not surprising. Fear of political excess was a central issue of the Revolution. The innovations in constitutional government at the state and national levels that emerged as a direct consequence of this concern represented the deepest, most long-lasting, and most important contribution that generation made— not only to America but to the political development of many new countries in the two centuries since 1776. The American colonial experience had taught that the exercise of public power, when unrestrained, was dangerous. Americans were more comfortable with private decision making, and they regarded the enhancement of private power as a necessary check on potential governmental abuse. This predilection resulted in the *privatization* of American law.[1]

Privatization presupposes that all individuals are equal before the law, that the law is neutral, and that the good of all is best promoted by shifting power from public bodies to private (preferably individual) actors. In reality, however, all individuals are not equal in relation to law, and collective action by individuals with common interests is inevitable. Privatization makes some sense in a perfectly individualized and atomized society; but in one where competing interests and

---

[1] The concept of privatization is receiving much current attention both in legal and general literature. See John R. LeClaire, "Public Wealth, Privatization, and the Constitution: The Alaska Example," *Boston University Law Review,* 61 (1981), 969–1006; T. Ohashi and T. Roth (eds.), *Privatization: Theory and Practice* (1980); Albert O. Hirschman, *Private Interest and Public Action* (Princeton, N.J., 1981).

pluralistic groupings jockey for power, privatization tends to substitute new forms of unchecked authority for older ones.

The American revolutionaries had perceived the threat to liberty as largely a problem of public power, and the revolutionary generation had fashioned legal remedies to deal with that problem. But no similar sensitivity to the challenge of private power in its many guises existed at the time of the Revolution. Thus while privatization extended the reach of human freedom in some respects, in others it had the effect of desensitizing Americans to the dangers posed by a class system based on sharp inequalities of wealth and power. Such inequalities were already much in evidence by the end of the colonial period. Thereafter, in the century following the Revolution, the problem of power and its control shifted from the public to the private sector. Social and, later, industrial exploitation replaced political abuse as the major challenge of American liberalism. But the ideological cast of the Revolution remained so strong that it took a revolution in political theory at the beginning of the twentieth century to devise new remedies to meet the threat to individual freedom and human dignity that the concentration of unchecked economic power in private hands then presented.

Long overlooked by historians, the leading social issue of the Revolutionary period was slavery and agitation for its abolition. Privatization manifested itself in liberalized procedures for personal manumission. Slave codes in most colonies made emancipation exceedingly difficult even for masters who wished to manumit their slaves either by *inter vivos* gift or by testamentary bequest. After the Revolution, however, even in the South, slave laws were eased, and increasing numbers of blacks achieved freedom through private acts of manumission.[2] Still, both in the North as well as the South, the law of slavery and freedom remained an area of primary concern to public law. But in the law of Church and State, in seditious libel law, and in criminal law privatization showed its effects with more dramatic force.

Church-State Law

The disestablishment of churches, a gradual and complex process in most of the original thirteen states, represented the fulfillment of a long-

[2] See Arthur Zilversmit, *The First Emancipation: The Abolition of Slavery in the North* (Chicago, 1967), pp. 18, 122–124, 155–190, *et passim*.

term tendency that had its beginnings in the colonial past. The notion that religion was a matter of public concern gradually gave way to a new attitude, which held that religious preference was a matter of private choice. Increasingly, Americans viewed the issue of religious belief, forms of religious practice, and differences over church governance as beyond the jurisdiction of public law. Rather, they conceived these to be problems of conscience, to be resolved in the give-and-take of private religious controversy. This was the central meaning of the movement to disestablish official, state churches in most of the colonies and in the early states. Roger Williams, that passionate seventeenth-century religious dissenter, first invented the metaphor of the "wall of separation" between the "garden" of the church and the "wilderness" of the state; but it was Thomas Jefferson, the leading figure of the eighteenth-century American Enlightenment, who put it best:

> The legitimate powers of government extend to such acts only as are injurious to others. But it does me no injury for my neighbor to say there are twenty gods, *or no god.* It neither picks my pocket nor breaks my leg.[3]

At the time of the Revolution, the question in most of the states was not whether there should be a single, established church such as the Congregational church in New England or the Anglican church in the South. The main issue was whether religion in general should be protected and supported by the state. While there was almost universal agreement that no single Christian church ought to occupy a favored position in public law, there was widespread disagreement over how far the separation of church and state should go.[4] Organized religion was thought to be an essential pillar of society. The state's civic responsibility to support religion in some way was equal in importance to its duty to maintain public health and domestic security. Learned teachers and ministers of the gospel were necessary to keep people from vice and to protect the social order from decay.

The essential question was how to keep religion part of the fabric of society without re-creating a religious establishment in the manner of the discredited colonial regime. Virginia's was the most radical response to this dilemma. There, the old Anglican (now Episcopalian) establish-

[3] Thomas Jefferson, *Notes on the State of Virginia,* ed. W. Peden (Chapel Hill, N.C., 1955), p. 159.
[4] Sidney E. Ahlstrom, *A Religious History of the American People* (New Haven, Conn., 1972), p. 380.

ment was closely identified with Loyalism. As a result, it did not have the kind of popular support that Congregationalism enjoyed in New England. Dissenter groups, Baptist and Presbyterians particularly, were located everywhere in Virginia, but their concentration in the western part of that state gave them a geographical base to mount an effective campaign of reform. Moreover, the leading political figures in Virginia, Thomas Jefferson and James Madison, were philosophically committed to complete separation of church and state. Consequently, there was a major confrontation in Virginia in the 1780s between separationists and those still anxious to maintain an alliance of church and state.

The two issues which brought that confrontation to a head were the incorporation of the Episcopal church and the so-called General Assessment Plan. The Church Incorporation Act of 1784 was a housekeeping measure whereby the property of the old Anglican establishment was put into the hands of reconstituted Episcopalian vestries. The vestries were democratized, church ministers were denied veto power over vestry decisions, and the commonwealth removed itself from further involvement in church governance. Nevertheless, deep opposition to the incorporation act persisted because it favored Episcopalian congregations over all others, and in 1786 the act providing for Episcopal incorporation was repealed.[5]

Even more controversial than incorporation, however, was the plan to tax every citizen for the support of the religious minister of the taxpayer's choice. The plan was a compromise measure that would provide for religion in general without singling out a particular church for preferential treatment. Each taxpayer could designate the church that was to receive the monies he was assessed. In the final version of the plan, those taxpayers who had no religious affiliations could earmark the funds collected for the support of "seminaries of learning" within the county.

Dissenter groups were divided over the general assessment. Presbyterians sided with Episcopalians, but Baptists remained opposed to any kind of compulsory religious tax, even one from which they stood to benefit. A major campaign was mounted to defeat the assessment, and James Madison's famous *Memorial and Remonstrance*,[6] which was widely circulated by his political allies in 1785, is generally credited with

[5] Thomas E. Buckley, S.J., *Church and State in Revolutionary Virginia, 1776–1787* (Charlottesville, Va., 1977), chaps. 3–5.
[6] See Document 9.

accomplishing its defeat in the fall of 1785. The opponents of the assessment plan, led by Jefferson and Madison, went on to consolidate their victory by enacting the Bill for Establishing Religious Freedom, which Jefferson had authored back in 1779. First presented to the Virginia legislature as part of the Revisal of the Laws (a general scheme of law reform), the Religious Freedom Bill was finally enacted into law in 1786.[7] It was the most far-reaching statute of its kind. For all practical purposes, the act destroyed the vestiges of the old Anglican religious establishment in Virginia for all time.

Disestablishment was a movement that affected the entire country in the aftermath of the Revolution, but in Virginia disestablishment meant more than just local control. The whole thrust of the Madisonian attack on the general assessment plan was that religion was a matter for the private "conscience of every man." Separation of church and state, disestablishment, religious freedom, and the right of "conscience"— these were central themes in the religious and legal history of the postrevolutionary era. Modern, twentieth-century efforts to define "zones of privacy"[8] owe much to the religious experience of the late eighteenth century. Religion was the first such zone, the first major sphere where public law was privatized.

The Law of the Press

Privatization also affected freedom of the press and the changing definition of seditious libel law in the 1790s and the early decades of the nineteenth century. In the eighteenth century, to criticize the government—or indeed anyone in authority—was a criminal offense.[9] To do so was to invite prosecution and the possibility of fine or imprisonment. The only question to be decided by a jury in a seditious libel case was a question of *fact*—did the writer or printer accused of publishing the offensive material actually publish it? If the jury's answer to that question was yes, then the accused was guilty of the offense charged. The judge's role was to decide, as a matter of *law,* whether or not the material in question was seditious. The fact that the offensive publication might be true was of no consequence.

[7] See Document 10.
[8] For example, *Griswold v. Connecticut,* 381 U.S. 479 (1965).
[9] Leonard W. Levy, *Legacy of Suppression: Freedom of Speech and Press in Early American History* (Cambridge, Mass., 1960), chaps. 1-2.

As Sir William Blackstone put it in explaining the English view of this common law crime, "(I)t is immaterial ... whether the matter of it be true or false, since the provocation, and not the falsity, is the thing to be punished criminally." As for the liberty of the press, said Blackstone, it "consists in laying no *previous* restraints upon publications, and not in freedom from censure for criminal matter when published."[10] In short, a printer was free to publish without fear of "prior restraint" through censorship or licensing laws, but he had to expect to be penalized by fine or imprisonment should a court of law find the publication seditious.

The case of John Peter Zenger, publisher of the *New York Weekly Journal,* in 1735 is one of the landmarks in the development of press freedom in America.[11] Zenger's acquittal represented an important change in seditious libel law, in that it established a precedent for the right of a jury to decide not only the fact of publication but the legal issue as well—that is, whether or not the material published was seditious. The Zenger case established that the truth of the statements contained in the suspect publication could be offered in evidence as a defense to the charge.

The Zenger case marked a breakthrough in the prevailing theory of seditious libel law. But not until the end of the century did Zengerian principles become firmly established in law. Ironically, it was the Sedition Act, passed in 1798 as part of a program of Federalist repression against the Jeffersonian opposition party, that codified these new legal doctrines by statute. The Sedition Act enlarged the role of the jury and allowed truth as a defense in libel actions.[12] It soon became evident, however, that Zengerian principles no longer provided adequate protection against governmental repression. First, making truth a defense in a seditious libel case merely meant that seditious libel was no longer a strict liability crime. The Sedition Act made truth an "affirmative defense" which put the burden of proving truth upon the defendant. But how could charges of corruption, incompetence, or ineffectiveness, the normal subjects of political debate, be proved? Open, vigorous, and healthy political discourse simply does not lend

---

[10] William Blackstone, *Commentaries on the Laws of England,* 4 vols. (1765–1769), vol. 4, p. 151.
[11] Stanley N. Katz (ed.)., *James Alexander's Brief Narrative of the Case and Trial of John Peter Zenger, Printer of the New York Weekly Journal* (Cambridge, Mass., 1963), pp. 1–35.
[12] See Document 12. See also James M. Smith, *Freedom's Fetters: The Alien and Sedition Laws and American Civil Liberties* (Ithaca, N.Y., 1956), chap. 18.

itself to analysis on a true-false standard. Political truth to one person is errant nonsense to another. Moreover, Federalist appointees to the new federal district courts were highly partisan and their jury charges in seditious libel cases were so pro-prosecution as to make guilty verdicts practically inevitable.[13] As a result the federal government was able to win a significant number of well-publicized cases under the Sedition Act despite the act's liberalization of seditious libel law. Consequently, after 1798 liberal writers began to challenge the whole concept of seditious libel on the grounds that it was a remnant of British monarchism. Liberals attacked the Sedition Act as an affront to the First Amendment to the Constitution, and seditious libel as ill-suited to a republican system of government, where the rulers are answerable to the people. Criticism of the people's representatives could not be illegitimate in a free society. These bold attacks on the law of seditious libel reinforced an emerging acceptance of political parties as a legitimate feature of political life in a free society.[14] Political parties were increasingly perceived as voluntary, private associations outside the realm of governmental interference.[15] This "privatization" of political life was closely associated with the decline in seditious libel prosecutions and the liberalization of libel law with which the Sedition Act was so ironically connected.

The radical critique of seditious libel did not prevail immediately, however. On the state level, where all criminal libel cases occurred after expiration of the infamous federal Sedition Act, public prosecutors still sought convictions on the basis of the old Blackstonian common-law formulations. *Commonwealth v. Clap* is an example of such a conviction.[16] The case involved an alleged libel against a minor public official. Defense counsel argued that since "every citizen may be considered as a candidate for public office," therefore everyone's character was "fair game" thus anticipating the modern constitutional doctrine of the "public figure."[17] While Chief Justice Parsons of the Massachusetts Supreme Judicial Court was not prepared to go this far, he

[13] One of the most notorious offenders was Justice Samuel Chase of the United States Supreme Court who, sitting as a circuit judge, charged the jury in *United States v. Thomas Cooper*, 25 Fed. Cas. 631 (Cir. Ct. Dist. Pa. 1800).
[14] Leonard W. Levy (ed.), *Freedom of the Press from Zenger to Jefferson* (New York, 1966), introduction.
[15] Richard Hofstadter, *The Idea of a Party System: The Rise of Legitimate Opposition in the United States, 1788-1840* (Berkeley, Calif., 1970), pp. 70-71.
[16] See Document 13.
[17] *New York Times v. Sullivan*, 376 U.S. 254 (1964); *Curtis Publishing Co. v. Butts*, 388 U.S. 130 (1967). These cases have established that "public officials" and "public figures" have a more difficult burden of proof in a libel action than do ordinary citizens.

did distinguish between elected and appointed officials. In the case of elected officials, liberal rules—such as truth as a defense—would be permitted. But in the case of a libel against an appointed official, private reputation would receive greater protection and truth would not be allowed. Since Clap had attacked an appointed official, the public auctioneer, the Court allowed his conviction to stand.

In a number of jurisdictions, most notably New York and Massachusetts, state legislatures enacted statutes that so changed the law of libel in the next several decades that criminal libel cases became a rarity after 1820, thereby indicating an overall decline in government interest in curbing subversive publications.[18] This net reduction in official intervention in public discourse may be interpreted as another instance of the privatization theme that runs through much of American legal history in the postrevolutionary period. To be sure, civil libel remained a subject of continuing importance. Nevertheless, by the mid-nineteenth century, the days when prosecutors went after writers, publishers, and printers for their seditious utterances had passed.[19] Not until the twentieth century has the United States government again made serious efforts to suppress freedom of the press. During the Vietnam War, for example, the government tried and failed to prevent *The New York Times* from publishing a documentary history of that war prepared by the Department of Defense.[20] More recently the Central Intelligence Agency has successfully forced a former CIA agent to submit nonclassified material concerning the agency for prepublication review. In upholding this restriction on activity which in another context would clearly come under First Amendment protection, the Supreme Court has fashioned what dissenting Justice John Paul Stevens called a "drastic new...species of prior restraint on a citizen's right to criticize his government."[21]

---

[18] Harold Nelson (ed.), *Freedom of the Press: From Hamilton to the Warren Court* (Indianapolis, Ind., 1967). pp. xix-1; Norman L. Rosenberg, "The Law of Political Libel and Freedom of Press in Nineteenth-Century America: An Interpretation," *American Journal of Legal History,* 17(1973), 336–352.

[19] For a discussion of the reasons for the decline in criminal libel prosecutions and civil suits against the press after 1825, see Rosenberg, "The Law of Political Libel and Freedom of Press."

[20] See the Pentagon Papers Case, *New York Times Co. v. United States,* 403 U.S. 713 (1971).

[21] See *Snepp v. United States,* 444 U.S. 507 (1980).

Moral Offenses

In the field of criminal law enforcement, prosecutors have wide discretion in deciding who is to be prosecuted, for which kinds of crime, and with what degree of vigor. In the postrevolutionary period, prosecutions for crimes against property and persons increased, whereas prosecutorial interest in offenses against morality—sexual offenses in particular—began to wane.[22]

For example, prosecutions for fornication, in both secular courts and church courts, were very high in the middle of the eighteenth century; but such prosecutions declined steadily in the 1780s and 1790s despite the fact that illicit fornication was still quite pervasive in America. The premarital pregnancy rate is one measure of this form of moral deviance after the Revolution. Table 1 demonstrates that premarital pregnancy remained high until about the middle of the nineteenth century. It shows the percentage of "first births" (i.e., first child born to a married couple) that occurred in less than 6 months, in less than 8½ months, and in less than 9 months of formal marriage. The figures clearly indicate a trend of increasing premarital pregnancy rates before 1800 and then a dramatic drop in those rates until 1880. Table 2 gives data on the disciplinary actions taken by Massachusetts churches between 1620 and 1840 in enforcing the law against illicit fornication. The peak period of enforcement came in the decades preceding the Revolution, with a dramatic drop in the last years of the eighteenth century, precisely the time when the premarital pregnancy rate—as shown in Table 1—was highest. While evidence derived from the numbers of cases appearing in church courts must be used with caution because of a steady decline in ecclesiastical disciplinary process in the postrevolutionary period,[23] studies of prosecution patterns in the regular secular courts support similar conclusions.[24] Clearly the decline in prosecutions was not due to a lower incidence of fornication. Rather,

---

[22] William E. Nelson, *Americanization of the Common Law: The Impact of Legal Change on Massachusetts Society, 1760-1830* (Cambridge, Mass., 1975), chaps. 3 and 6, passim; and Nelson, "Emerging Notions of Modern Criminal Law in the Revolutionary Era: An Historical Perspective," *New York University Law Review,* 42 (1967), 450–482.

[23] William E. Nelson, *Dispute and Conflict Resolution in Plymouth County, Massachusetts, 1725-1825* (Chapel Hill, 1981), p. 150.

[24] See, for example, Michael S. Hindus, *Prison and Plantation: Crime, Justice, and Authority in Massachusetts and South Carolina, 1767-1878* (Chapel Hill, 1980), pp. 48-51, *et passim.*

Table 1
Premarital Pregnancy in America: First Births Occurring in Less
Than 6, 8½, and 9 Months After Marriage

	Less than 6 Months		Under 8½ Months		Under 9 Months	
	%	N	%	N	%	N
–1680	3.3	511	6.8	511	8.1	663
1681–1720	6.7	445	14.1	518	12.1	1156
1721–1760	9.9	881	21.2	1146	22.5	1442
1761–1800	16.7	970	27.2	1266	33.0	1097
1801–1840	10.3	573	17.7	815	23.7	616
1841–1880	5.8	572	9.6	467	12.6	572
1881–1910	15.1	119	23.3	232	24.4	119

Source: Adapted from D.S. Smith and M.S. Hindus, "Premarital Pregnancy in America, 1640-1971: An Overview and Interpretation," *Journal of Interdisciplinary History,* 5 (1975), p. 561, by permission of the *Journal of Interdisciplinary History* and the M.I.T. Press, Cambridge, Mass. Copyright © 1975 by the Massachusetts Institute of Technology Press and the editors of the *Journal of Interdisciplinary History.*

Table 2
Fornication Cases in Massachusetts Churches (by County),
1620-1840

	1620-1689	1690-1729	1730-1769	1770-1809	1810-1840
Plymouth	4	9	64	29	3
Barnstable	6	5	71	10	0
Norfolk	3	25	90	20	0
Suffolk	28	41	30	11	2
Essex	15	67	120	36	1
Middlesex	1	30	134	44	0
Worcester	0	1	32	19	1
Hampshire	0	9	133	96	13
Berkshire	0	0	5	25	11
Total	57	187	679	290	31

Source: Derived from Emil Oberholzer, Jr., *Delinquent Saints: Disciplinary Action in the Early Congregational Churches of Massachusetts* (New York, 1956), pp. 254-255.

it suggests a dramatic drop in prosecutorial attention to sexual immorality even by church courts, which in turn suggests that society was beginning to recognize that certain forms of private behavior between consenting adults should no longer be the primary concern of the criminal law.

Criminal law reformers had begun to apply rationalistic and utilitarian measures to the social analysis of crime and punishment.[25] Differentiating between public and private offenses was clearly part of this movement. The law remained nominally opposed to the same kinds of behavioral deviations as in the past. Statutes against adultery, fornication and bastardy were not repealed. Prosecutions for blasphemy continued into the 1830s. Nevertheless, these kinds of offenses were in areas that the law increasingly viewed as within the sphere of private life and, therefore, beyond the legitimate reach of the criminal process.

To freedom of conscience and freedom of political expression and association, then, must be added the growing freedom of sexual expression—another manifestation of the effects of legal privatization. In short, in sharp contrast with the colonial past, government in the postrevolutionary period was becoming less activist in seeking to monitor religious, political, and moral behavior.

[25] Virginia, Bill for Proportioning Crimes and Punishments in Cases Heretofore Capital (1779), in *The Papers of Thomas Jefferson,* Julian P. Boyd (ed.), 19 vols. to date (Princeton, N.J., 1950–), vol. 2, pp. 492–507. The work of the early Italian criminologist Cesare Bonesana (1738–1794), marchese di Beccaria [Beccaria], *Crimes and Punishments (Dei delitti e delle pene)* (Milan, 1764), was widely translated, and his ideas were implemented in many reform-minded Western countries, including the United States. The work of the English utilitarian philosopher Jeremy Bentham (1748–1832) was also important to early American criminology and law reform.

3

The Private Law

In the development of an "American jurisprudence" responsive to the special circumstances of American life, legislative bodies and courts of law had to mold both statutory law and case law to the standard of a written constitution. American law in this formative period of its modern growth was rooted in two very different sources. The first was a positivist tradition, going back to the colonial period, which stood for the proposition that law was an instrument to be used to meet social demands and exigent circumstances. The second was a natural-law tradition embodied in the written constitutionalism of the revolutionary period itself, which held that there were certain fundamental principles or laws of nature which antedated the legal regime and to which statutes and judicial decisions had to conform. Constitutions were enacted to codify these antecedent natural-law and natural-rights principles, and lawmakers and judges were bound within this constitutional framework.[1]

Caught in the tension between positive law and natural law, between economic power and constitutional values, state legislatures required high appellate courts to give reasoned explanations of the logic that led to particular results in particular cases. State legislatures also provided for the appointment of official court reporters to publish these opinions for the guidance of lower courts and legal practitioners.[2] Out of these

---

[1] Gordon S. Wood, *The Creation of the American Republic, 1776–1787* (Chapel Hill, N.C., 1969), pp. 291–305.
[2] See, for example, 3 Laws of the Commonwealth of Massachusetts (1804), p. 227. See also Lawrence M. Friedman, *A History of American Law* (New York, 1973), pp. 282–285.

reports a body of case law emerged and with it the doctrine of "binding precedent."[3] The emergence of this body of decided cases meant that American courts were in the process of developing a distinctively American common law. In the 1820s, 1830s and 1840s treatise writers systematized this body of American law in a remarkable series of books that finally ended the dependence of the American legal profession on English legal learning.[4] In addition, state and federal courts assumed the power of judicial review whereby appellate courts heard challenges to statutes, executive orders, and lower court rulings and decided them according to the standard of the written constitution at either the state or the federal level.[5] Judicial review was a uniquely American institution. Under the power of judicial review courts of law resolved basic social conflicts within a framework of law.

Although the Revolution ushered in a period of growth and change in public law, particularly in the field of constitutional law, there is no doubt that the greatest growing point in the legal system was in the field of private law. Here, policy judgments of the courts had substantial effects upon the values, groups, and interests that competed for legal recognition. These policy judgments often had one-sided effects. Law played a critical role in distributing resources, in allocating costs and benefits in the process of economic development, and in encouraging the organization of certain economic groupings, such as corporations, while discouraging others, such as the early trade unions. This is not to argue with reductionist logic that legal authorities, courts in particular, mechanically enforced the will of favored special interests, economic developers, or entrepreneurs in new commercial markets. Rather, the courts acted as mediating bodies among conflicting political forces and changing value systems. If the overall thrust of legal policy in the period favored venture capital over established wealth, corporations over labor unions, milldam owners over simple farmers, this was because of an emerging ideological consensus that preferred growth to stability,

---

[3] Harold J. Berman and William R. Greiner, *The Nature and Functions of Law* (New York, 1966), pp. 491–494 ("The Historical Development of the Doctrine of Precedent").
[4] Leading examples of the early nineteenth-century treatise are James Kent, *Commentaries on American Law,* 4 vols. (1826–1830); Joseph Story, *Equity Jurisprudence* (1835); Theodore Sedgwick, *Treatise on the Measure of Damages* (1847). For a discussion of the treatise-writing tradition, see Roscoe Pound, *The Formative Era of American Law* (Boston, 1938), chap. 4.
[5] William E. Nelson, "Changing Conceptions of Judicial Review: The Evolution of Constitutional Theory in the States, 1790–1860," *University of Pennsylvania Law Review,* 120 (1972), 1166–1185.

action to inaction, and risk to certainty, and that favored individual initiative, choice, and decision over community custom, old values, and social consensus.[6]

Private Property and Legal Takings

Eminent domain law, still in its infancy in the immediate postrevolutionary period, already reflected many of the forces pushing and pulling American law in new directions. Although few of the state constitutions adopted in the revolutionary era contained just compensation provisions, the principle was widely recognized: private property could not be appropriated for public use unless the owner was compensated for the taking.[7] The Fifth Amendment to the Constitution put it most succinctly: "nor shall private property be taken for public use without just compensation."[8] The words are simple and straightforward. Even in states with no expressed constitutional provision for just compensation, courts adopted the federal constitutional provision or applied compensation law either as an equitable remedy or by reason of natural justice. Yet despite its "just compensation" predicate, eminent domain became one of the most fertile areas for the undermining of the absolute right to private property. Indeed, the "devolution" of the eminent domain power to "private takers" eroded absolutist conceptions of private property to such an extent that eminent domain law can be said to have prepared the way for the regulatory state.[9]

The difficult questions of eminent domain law were not subject to automatic resolution by reference to fundamental constitutional sources or to simple principles of compensation. Did milldam owners who raised a head of water in order to operate a waterwheel subject an upstream neighbor to an involuntary taking when the latter's land was flooded? Was such a taking by a private party equally compensable as when the taking was by public authority? Did the construction of a milldam constitute a benefit sufficient to satisfy a "public use" test?

[6] James Willard Hurst, *Law and the Conditions of Freedom in the Nineteenth-Century United States* (Madison, Wis., 1964).
[7] Morton J. Horwitz, *The Transformation of American Law: 1780–1860* (Cambridge, Mass., 1977), pp. 63–66.
[8] U.S. Constitution, Amend. V.
[9] See Harry N. Scheiber, "Property Law, Expropriation, and Resource Allocation by Government, 1789–1910," *Journal of Economic History,* 33 (1973), 323.

What if the person whose land was flooded also benefited from the taking? Was his benefit to be "offset" against his loss? How was compensation to be paid, in kind or in money, and if in money, what would be the appropriate measure of damages?[10]

These were serious issues not easily resolved and often not settled in ways indicated by constitutional provisions. In Massachusetts, for example, the 1780 constitution declared that "whenever ... publick exigencies require that the property of any individual should be appropriated to public uses, he shall receive a reasonable compensation therefor."[11] In *Commonwealth v. Sessions of Middlesex* (1812), however, the Supreme Judicial Court decided that when private land was taken for a public road, if the proprietor's benefit from the construction of the road exceeded his damage from the taking, then no compensation was due because there was no loss.[12] Takings such as this, despite judicial sanction, were recognized as confiscatory by at least some offended contemporaries. As the reporter of the *Middlesex* case noted:

> [T]he justice of the rule is certainly very questionable. The expense of making a highway is a common burden, incurred for the common good; of which burden, each citizen, in proportion to his ability, ordinarily sustains his part, and if one accidentally, whether by dwelling or having his lands near the highway, or from any other circumstance, derives more benefit from it than another, this does not seem to afford any sound reason for imposing a heavier tax upon him merely on that account. Indeed, it would be impracticable, in taxation, to apply the rule generally, and assess the expenses of public works upon each citizen in exact proportion to the supposed benefit he may be expected to derive from them. *Where, then, is the equality or justice of applying the rule in a case like that reported in the text* [emphasis added]?[13]

Thus, courts upheld small individual proprietors against powerful interests when it was not at all clear that the "taking" would result in a genuine public benefit. For example, a Massachusetts case held that

> ... where private persons or corporations prevail on towns to layout town ways, colorably for the use of the inhabitants, but really for their own

---

[10] For further discussion of milldam law, see Horwitz, *Transformation of American Law*, pp. 47–53.

[11] Massachusetts Constitution, Declaration of Rights (1780), Art. X.

[12] *Commonwealth v. Sessions of Middlesex*, 9 Mass. 388 (1812).

[13] Id. at 389n.

32   *Law in the New Republic*

benefit, over lands of others who are opposed to the way...a jury may discontinue a way thus irregularly obtained; and they ought to do it, whenever they are satisfied that private emolument, and not the interest of the inhabitants, has caused the way to be located.[14]

The emerging ideological commitment to economic growth and development, which the extension of the power of eminent domain enhanced, created a tension with the equally strong social imperative to prevent the abuse of the eminent domain power for purely private ends. The devolution of eminent domain from public authority to private actors was a trend that greatly accelerated after the middle of the nineteenth century; but the trend had begun in the generation following the Revolution, a time when consciousness of the natural rights basis of American constitutionalism was most keenly felt and understood. In short, while the law clearly moved in directions that promoted growth, the law did not simply ratify all of the demands of favored economic interests. Rather it mediated between conflicting values and competing social goods.

Traditional property rights such as quiet enjoyment and just compensation were subjected to other challenges besides the expanded usage of the eminent domain power. Internal improvements and changing technologies necessarily brought values and interests into new sorts of conflicts. If property owners in the eighteenth century enjoyed settled traditions of just compensation and the right to peaceable possession, the opening of the nineteenth century witnessed a growing number of modifications of these customary rules, as builders of roads, canals, bridges, buildings, and mills increasingly interfered with other people's property. The classic example of this development occurred in Massachusetts, a just compensation state whose law was transformed in this period into an instrument for the promotion of economic growth.[15] In 1795 the Massachusetts General Court (the state legislature) passed a milldam act that set up a procedure for compensating riparian landowners whose lands were flooded when a neighbor constructed a dam in order to work a waterwheel.[16] This statute provided for the payment of yearly damages, the damages to be appraised by a jury. The effect of the act was to force a complainant to lease away part of his land

[14] *Commonwealth v. Cambridge,* 7 Mass. 158 (1810).
[15] Morton J. Horwitz, "The Emergence of an Instrumental Conception of Law," in *Law in American History,* ed. by D. Fleming and B. Bailyn (Boston, 1971), pp. 287–326.
[16] See Document 14.

in return for an annual rent for as long as the millowner wished to flood. Not only was the plaintiff thereby deprived of the use of his own land, but the award of an annuity rather than a lump sum payment meant that, too often, plaintiffs so situated could not reinvest in alternative resources; nor did they get compensation, in years when no flooding occurred, for the permanent damage to the value of their land.

An important decision of the Massachusetts Supreme Judicial Court, *Stowell v. Flagg,* established that the procedure for awarding annual damages under the 1795 enactment was to be the exclusive remedy. Plaintiffs whose lands were flooded were barred from resorting to more normal legal remedies such as self-help, suits at law for trespass or nuisance, or a petition for injunctive relief.[17] Under self-help, the property owner whose quiet enjoyment had been disturbed could go onto someone else's land and remove the disturbance. Such action would not constitute the wrong of trespass (a serious *intentional tort*) because the complainant had justification. Thus a property owner whose lands were flooded by a neighbor's dam could destroy the dam without incurring liability. At law, such a plaintiff had an alternative remedy, a suit in trespass or nuisance. If the suit were in trespass, the claim to damages would not be limited to the actual value of the loss because the law would seek to deter as well as to compensate. Similarly in a nuisance action, the damages awarded might be higher than the loss. A North Carolina decision summarized the reasons why damages for nuisance ought not to be either light or merely compensatory; the same reasoning would of course apply to the punitive damages available in trespass:

> ... [I]f the keeping up of the nuisance will afford more profit to the wrongdoer than the small damages assessed by a jury, he will keep it up forever; and thus one individual will be enabled to take from another his property against his consent, and detain it from him as long as he pleases. The damages ought not to be for what the incommoded property is worth, but competent to the purpose in view; that is, a demolition of the erection that occasions the nuisance. Sometimes the profits of such erections as merchant mills for instance, are of much greater value in one year, than the

[17] See Document 15. *Self-help* is the taking of an action by an aggrieved party to remedy a wrong without use of the legal process. A *suit at law* is a civil action undertaken in accordance with established rules of civil procedure, seeking damages as the remedy. *Injunctive relief* is an equitable remedy granted by a court at the instance of a party plaintiff against a party defendant, forbidding the latter from doing an act that will cause irreparable injury to the complaining party.

fee simple of the annoyed property. In such cases the object of the law cannot be obtained but by damages equivalent to the profits gained by the erection, or by damages to such an amount as will render those profits not worth pursuing.[18]

Finally, a flooded riparian, under ordinary circumstances, could petition for an injunction blocking either construction of the dam or the millowner's usage of his mill if that disturbed the plaintiff's quiet enjoyment. But the Massachusetts Milldam Act, instead of preserving the *plaintiff's prospective remedy* for preventing damage (i.e., through the injunction), authorized *prospective takings* by the millowner. This represented a major departure from the practice followed in a number of other states where statutes required prior authorization for each dam before it was constructed.[19] Even more significantly, the Milldam Act of 1795, in conjunction with the Supreme Judicial Court's decision in *Stowell v. Flagg,* signified a fundamental incursion into traditional notions about the right to private property.

This departure from customary understandings did not escape the concern of contemporaries. One critic of *Stowell v. Flagg* questioned whether such an "unusual and extraordinary provision of the law" could be constitutional:

> I may not seize my neighbor's goods, except by process of law, against his consent, even though I may offer him their full value in return. I may not plough my neighbor's land, even though the thorn and the thistle alone flourish there under the sluggish husbandry of its owner. I may not obscure the light from the ancient cottage window, though poverty and weakness alone may have enjoyed its cheerful influence; nor may I poison the water or air that has, for years, given health and comfort to my neighbor, though the trade I may follow would enrich my coffers, and accommodate the neighborhood. But the ordinary rules of right and wrong, as to the enjoyment of private property, seem not to apply to estates which border upon any of the beautiful and healthy streams which enliven our scenery. They may be sacrificed to the speculating spirit of the manufacturer.[20]

The fundamental right to property guaranteed by the state and federal constitutions was the right not to have property taken even for public use without consent. Unconsented taxation, after all, was the triggering

---

[18] *Bradley v. Amis,* 3 N.C. 399 (1806).
[19] Horwitz, *Transformation of American Law,* p. 48.
[20] Joseph K. Angell, "The Law of Water Privileges," *American Jurist,* 2 (1829), 25.

cause of the American Revolution. In this case, however, the law authorized a taking for private use and deprived owners of property "without due process of law." As this writer continued: Through the mill act and *Stowell v. Flagg* the law authorized "the occupation and enjoyment of another's estate *forever;* which . . . is altogether unlike any other assumption of private property usually contemplated by our constitutions."

The Law of Negligence

Perhaps the most important development of the private law in the nineteenth century was the emergence of negligence as a limitation on liability for injuries to persons and property.[21] The eighteenth century was a period when plaintiffs were compensated under a system of strict liability.[22] Under strict liability, defendants were liable in damages for having caused loss or injury even if they were not at fault or negligent for having failed to observe reasonable precautions. People acted at their risk, and if their action caused loss, then aggrieved plaintiffs would be compensated. In the early nineteenth century however, the regime of strict liability began to break down. Social values were in transition; action was now to be encouraged, not penalized, and devices were needed to shield risk takers from liability. The burden was put on the injured party to establish that the defendant had acted negligently or carelessly. If the plaintiff failed to carry that burden, then the law deemed the loss to have been accidental and it "must lie where it falls"— that is, on the injured plaintiff. In a negligence regime, plaintiffs were to become "self-insurers."[23]

In the age of strict liability, negligence had generally meant *neglect* of a duty imposed by office, contract, or status.[24] If a town failed to keep up a bridge or road, and if someone was injured as a result, the liability was not determined on the basis of carelessness but for nonperformance of

[21] *Negligence* is the failure to do some act that a reasonable or prudent person would do, or the doing of an act that a reasonable or prudent person would not do, under similar circumstances.

[22] In *strict liability*, the plaintiff does not have to show that the defendant was at fault or was negligent, but only that the defendant did the act which caused the injury.

[23] *Self-insurance* means simply that the injured party must bear any loss suffered; the law will not distribute the loss through "social cost spreading" or some other system of relief.

[24] Horwitz, *Transformation of American Law,* pp. 85–87.

the duty imposed by law to maintain the facility. So, for example, if a prisoner escaped from a jailhouse, the sheriff was usually found to have "neglected" his official duty of safekeeping even if he had not acted carelessly in the performance of his office. But the negligence standard that emerged by the middle of the nineteenth century would mean something else—not neglect but fault, misfeasance, or failure to observe some "standard of care"; a failure on the part of the defendant that the plaintiff had to prove in order to recover.

The shift from strict liability to negligence first occurred in cases where there were joint actors and where each party to the dispute had exposed the other to some risk or danger. Where there was such mutuality of risk or danger, the law would determine which party would bear responsibility for the injury or loss that resulted from the encounter. It did so by inquiring whose negligence was causative—in other words, which party was at fault. The earliest cases that raised these questions were collision cases involving ships moving in harbor, or travelers and stagecoaches on roadways.

Increasingly, the law confined the strict liability doctrine to those cases where the plaintiff had not exposed the defendant to a "reciprocity of risk." It is for this reason that the case of *Clark v. Foot* represents such a radical, even astonishing, departure from the old regime of strict liability.[25] Clark and Foot were neighbors. Foot set fire to some of his fallow land, and the fire spread, causing damage to Clark's property. Clark sued Foot and lost because he failed to prove that Foot (or his servant) had been careless or negligent. Interestingly enough, however, it is not a collision case with two joint actors but a land case where only the defendant was active while the plaintiff was passive. There was no question of causation. The plaintiff was disturbed in the quiet enjoyment of his property. But for the defendant's action, there would have been no loss. Yet, the plaintiff failed to recover. Moreover, the loss was caused by a spreading fire. Fire damage had always been and continued to be the classic instance for the application of the rule of absolute liability. Use of fire was lawful, but one used it at one's peril because fire is "inherently dangerous." In both English and American law, any damage caused by fire was compensable regardless of fault. The New York court's decision in *Clark v. Foot,* therefore, ran counter to an ancient rule of common law.

[25] See Document 16.

The emergence of the negligence doctrine in the nineteenth century, and the narrowing of absolute liability, corresponds to the privatization model observable in other areas of the developing law. Both in absolute liability and in negligence, a duty owed to the world was imposed by law. But in an absolute liability regime, the duty was highly generalized, external, and objective. Action was risky, for damage was compensable regardless of fault. In a regime governed by the negligence standard, however, the duty was confined, specified, and determined according to some standard of conduct to which the individual actor-defendant was expected to conform. Whether or not he had acted nonnegligently was a subjective judgment made relative to each person and to the circumstances of each case. To be sure, the law might impose a general "standard of care" as defined by reasonable or prudent persons (the jury), but the parameters of that standard were not determined by the law or by the community but by the customary conduct of actors in the same situation or occupation as the defendant. In fact in some cases, the standard of conduct was created by the defendant's own past record of conduct. Not action per se but deviation from an acceptable standard of action—defined either by the defendant or by actors similarly situated— gave rise to liability. In this sense, the standards of liability were privatized and narrowed.

Clark v. Foot foreshadowed the new theory of negligence that later was defined by the phrase: "there is no liability without fault." It is one of the first in what was to become a steady and swelling volume of cases in which plaintiffs would lose because they failed to prove the defendant's negligence to the satisfaction of courts and juries. In this sense the case is a turning point in American law. Thus the erosion of traditional property values, discussed above, coincided with the emergence of negligence law, which was soon to become an important limitation on liability. *Clark v. Foot* in New York and *Stowell v. Flagg* in Massachusetts were classic instances of old legal notions in the most ancient field of the common law—the law of real property—going through revolutionary changes under the impact of forces that the courts had only begun to perceive and had, as yet, but barely articulated.

Contract Law

Related transformations were also affecting the law of contracts. Under the chief justiceship of John Marshall, the Supreme Court of the

United States made the contract clause of the U.S. Constitution into a major force behind legal privatization. That clause prohibited any state from enacting a "law impairing the obligation of contracts."[26] With that provision, the Founding Fathers hoped to curb the more radical state legislatures from enacting the kind of debtor relief laws that had outraged creditors in the economic depression of the 1780s.[27] The early decisions interpreting the contract clause were applied, however, not to contracts between private parties but to state land grants to developers and charter grants to public corporations. The Supreme Court said that such grants were really contracts between the state and the grantee, and that legislation which altered the terms of a grant (or repealed it altogether) would adversely affect those property interests that might have vested under such a grant.[28] Legislation of this kind, therefore, was invalid under the contract clause of the federal constitution because of the consequent "impairment" of contractual obligations that the state itself had undertaken. While states later would protect their freedom of action by reserving authority to alter prospectively a legislative or charter grant, the effect of these early Supreme Court decisions was to liken the state to an ordinary private party.

Thus for the U.S. Supreme Court under John Marshall, the contract clause became a device for limiting state action—not merely when such action might interfere with private contractual relationships but also when the state itself was one of the contracting parties. Under such an interpretation of its meaning, the contract clause became an instrument for reducing the state to the status of a private party in order to prevent it from altering the terms of its grants and charters to private interests. Later cases would cut back on Marshall's broad interpretation of the contract clause.[29] But the privatization model remained deeply embedded in constitutional law. Privatization limited the exercise of state authority unless that exercise could be rationalized on the basis of the state's inherent police powers or of some other doctrine of public utility or need.[30]

---

[26] U.S. Constitution, Art. I, Sec. 10.
[27] Benjamin F. Wright, *Consensus and Continuity, 1776-1787* (New York, 1958), p. 53.
[28] See, for example, *Fletcher v. Peck* (Document 17) and *Dartmouth College v. Woodward,* 17 U.S. (4 Wheat.) 518 (1819).
[29] See, for example, *Ogden v. Saunders,* 25 U.S. (12 Wheat.) 213 (1827), and *Charles River Bridge v. Warren Bridge et al.,* 36 U.S. (11 Pet.) 420 (1837).
[30] Not until 1948 did the privatization model in contract law get turned on its head. In that year, the U.S. Supreme Court outlawed racially restrictive covenants in the sale of real property. In *Shelley v. Kraemer,* 334 U.S. 1 (1948), private decision makers were barred

In the early nineteenth century, contractual freedom was "privatized" in still other ways. The modern theory of contract law is that private individuals are lawmakers who, through the instrument of the bargained-for private agreement, create a legal regime which will govern their future conduct just as if that behavior had been conditioned by statute, regulation, or court order. Behind this "contract theory" stands the psychology of free will and the political philosophy of self-government: mature human beings in a free society are capable of ordering their affairs in ways they best understand.

This has not always been so. In the eighteenth century the law stood as a pervasive "omnipresence in the sky," particularly in the contract area. Parties could enter into a contract (or "covenant") only if the terms of their bargain did not violate group values, rules of social conduct, or community norms. The law of contracts was undeveloped, its rules were traditional, and its design fitted the mold of a stable, premodern society, where relationships were face to face, obligations were undertaken and discharged according to well-established customs, and deviations from the norm were controlled by carefully defined doctrines and procedures.[31]

A contract action brought by a Massachusetts physician a decade before the Revolution illustrates the old law. The doctor's bill was for drugs, travel costs, and medical attention, but not surprisingly, there was no written contract defining the terms of remuneration. Nevertheless, the court decided that these costs "had as fixed a Price as Goods sold by a Shopkeeper. . . . The jury did, according as the Law was laid down to them, and struck off about £7 from the Account, lowering the Charges, probably, to what they thought 'reasonable.'" The doctor's charges, in other words, were fixed by local custom as established by jurors drawn from the community, who knew what those customs were.[32]

But while many traditional elements of the old law of contracts persisted well into the nineteenth century, by 1820 that law showed signs

from performing acts that the Constitution prohibited the states from performing if such acts required state support or subvention, however indirect. In the early contract clause cases, state legislatures had had to shape their conduct as if they were private parties; but under the doctrine of "state action," as expanded by *Shelley v. Kraemer,* private parties were subjected to the requirements imposed on states and their instrumentalities.

[31] William E. Nelson, *Americanization of the Common Law: The Impact of Legal Change on Massachusetts Society, 1760–1830* (Cambridge, Mass., 1975), pp. 54–62.

[32] *Pynchon v. Brewster,* Quincy 224 (Mass. 1766). See Horwitz, *Transformation of American Law,* p. 165.

of rapid change in the direction of modern contract law. The deepest change was the shift away from community values and toward individual intent as the ultimate test of the enforceable agreement. The purpose of the developing rules of contract law was to carry out the will of the parties even when their agreements reflected judgments of value or mandated behavior or performance that ran contrary to accepted custom. For example, courts increasingly allowed the amount of "consideration"[33] to be determined by the parties. Even nominal amounts would be permitted if the parties so intended. This was in contrast to eighteenth century usage, where courts would not enforce contracts where the items exchanged had not been of roughly equivalent value.[34]

Powerful historical forces generated these changes in contract law. The new commercial economy was creating novel products, distant markets, and fluid price structures, plus a whole range of complex commercial relationships among buyers and sellers, employers and workers, producers and consumers. Shifting patterns of trade, the growth of commodity and "futures" markets, greater impersonality in the relations between contracting parties—all forced substantial changes in the rules that governed agreements. In addition, behind the demanding requirements of the new commerce and industry lurked the ideology of private decision making, an ideology rooted as much in political and social attitudes as in hard economic fact. On every level, postrevolutionary legal thought emphasized the lawmaking role of the private individual while it criticized the superintending power of the state. The private contract was, in essence, a private statute; the law of contracts facilitated "private ordering" of markets and resources. In a word, the private contract represented self-government in private law, just as republicanism promoted the representative principle in public law.[35]

The triumph of what has been called "the will theory of contracts" carried the republican impulse to the smallest unit in society—two individuals, who in concert formed a microlegislature and made law. Modern contract law theory brought Americans closer to direct democracy than did their representative political institutions. In practice, however, "liberty of contract" was based upon the illusion that

[33] *Consideration* is the benefit that accrues to the promisor or the loss incurred by the promisee in a bargained-for agreement.

[34] Horwitz, *Transformation of American Law*, chap. 6.

[35] Morton J. Horwitz, "The Historical Foundations of Modern Contract Law," *Harvard Law Review*, 87 (1974), 917–956.

parties entered into agreements on the basis of genuine negotiating equality. In fact the myth of "liberty of contract" eventually became part of an ideological justification for social and economic exploitation. The, theory of contracts was sound, but its implementation in a world where wealth and power were not equally distributed inevitably brought distortions in result not unlike the distortions in the legislative process that occurred when powerful interests, or lobbies, corrupted political institutions in the name of representative democracy.

The decline of the eighteenth century's "substantive theory of contracts" meant that the law concerned itself only with the formalities of contract formation. Neither the relative bargaining positions of the parties, nor the substance of what they agreed to was any longer a central issue. This opened the door to widespread abuse by the powerful over the weak, the informed against the ignorant, and too often, the rich against the poor. The emergence of modern contract theory in the nineteenth century was the clearest expression of the tendency of American law to ratify underlying social relationships. Of all the branches of the legal system, the law of contracts became the least responsive to the demands of social justice and economic equality.

The Private Corporation

The rise of the will theory of contracts also contributed to the development of the modern American business corporation. The public corporation was an old legal institution. The oldest example was the municipality incorporated by the sovereign—in England by the king-in-Parliament, and in America after independence, by the state legislatures. Still another form of public corporation was the joint stock company. Many of the original American colonies, such as the Plymouth colony, the Massachusetts Bay colony and early Virginia were established and settled in this way. Joint stock companies pooled the financial resources of participating adventurers in order to promote England's expansion overseas. While these public corporate entities were largely self-governing in day-to-day operations, the power of the government to alter their corporate charters and to reach the personal assets of the individual shareholders was unlimited.[36]

[36] Joseph S. Davis, *Essays in the Earlier History of American Corporations,* 2 vols. (New York, 1965), Essay 1 (chaps. 1–5).

But the law of corporations went through significant transformations in the period after the American Revolution. Chief among these was the concept of limited liability: individual assets would no longer be liable to cover the debts of the corporation unless the member shareholders had so agreed. The intentions of the parties governed this critical aspect of corporate life—a significant departure from earlier practice, wherein the obligations of the members were determined by their status as corporate shareholders rather then by the contractual relationship between each shareholder and the corporation. This transformation in the law of corporations is an instance of Sir Henry Maine's famous generalization about the evolution of modern law in "progressive societies," which he characterized as "a movement from status to contract."[37] The law now prevented forced assessments against shareholders by the corporation, by corporate creditors or by public authorities. The corporation thereby became a private, voluntary association of a most unusual kind.[38]

In place of the public purposes that public corporations had asserted as the primary justification for their special legal status, the new private corporations of the nineteenth century utilized new theories of political economy which held that indirect public benefit was best achieved through the pursuit of private gain. Adam Smith, the great Scottish philosopher and founder of modern political economy, supplied the ideological basis for this proposition. In his *Wealth of Nations,* first published in 1776, the year of American independence, Smith advanced the novel notion that the public good was best promoted not by disinterested individual "virtue" but through harnessing the passion for private gain.

> [E]very individual necessarily labours to render the annual revenue of the society as great as he can. He generally, indeed, neither intends to promote the public interest, nor knows how much he is promoting it. By preferring the support of domestic to that of foreign industry, he intends only his own security; and by directing that industry in such a manner as its produce may be of the greatest value, he intends only his own gain, and he is in this, as in many other cases, *led by an invisible hand to promote an end which was not part of his intention.* By pursuing his own interest he frequently promotes that of the society more effectually than when he really intends to promote it. [emphasis added][39]

[37] Sir Henry Maine, *Ancient Law* (London, 1930; originally published 1861), p. 18.
[38] See Horwitz, *Transformation of American Law,* pp. 111–114; and Nelson, *Americanization of the Common Law,* pp. 133–136.
[39] Adam Smith, *The Wealth of Nations,* 6th ed., 2 vols. (London, 1950), vol. 1, p. 421.

Smith's metaphor of the *invisible hand* had a profound impact on America, where entrepreneurs increasingly asserted the principle of the free market and competition over monopoly privilege.

The major legal victory which the new private corporations won in America in the period after the Revolution was the establishment as a principle of constitutional jurisprudence that corporations had legal standing and were entitled to the same legal protections and constitutional guarantees as individuals. In the *Dartmouth College Case*[40], Chief Justice Marshall held that the New Hampshire state legislature, in amending the corporate charter granted to the original trustees of Dartmouth College had impaired the contractual obligation of the state to the trustees in violation of the contract clause. Marshall's holding that a corporate charter was simply a contract had been suggested by earlier decisions[41] but never enunciated as a doctrine of constitutional law. With more force than justification Marshall simply stated that a "charter is a contract" and thereby radically altered the status of corporations in American law. Commercial corporations, in particular, benefited from this landmark decision. The decision transformed the contract clause, which had been designed by the framers of the Constitution to protect individual property rights, into an instrument for the benefit of the business corporation, which was already becoming the most dynamic form of private aggrandizement of wealth and power in America. Associate Justice Joseph Story's concurring opinion further contributed to the division of corporate entities into private corporations and public corporations. According to Story, a corporate charter granted by the state to achieve a public purpose, whether to build a road, dig a canal, or establish a bank, was nonetheless private if the corporate stock was privately owned.[42]

But private corporations held onto their quasi-public character when it was convenient to do so. For example, when an established corporation wanted to block new competitors, or when a turnpike company wished to exercise eminent domain power in order to secure a right-of-way, it was useful to claim that the corporation was an arm of public authority, that it was established for a public purpose, and that it was entitled to special protections. While such claims came under

---

[40] *Dartmouth College v. Woodward*, 17 U.S. (4 Wheat.) 518 (1819).
[41] *Fletcher v. Peck*, 10 U.S. (6 Cranch) 87 (1810), *New Jersey v. Wilson*, 11 U.S. (7 Cranch) 164 (1812), *Terrett v. Taylor*, 13 U.S. (9 Cranch) 43 (1815).
[42] Francis N. Stites, *Private Interest and Public Gain: The Dartmouth College Case, 1819* (Amherst, Mass., 1972), chaps. 7, 9.

mounting criticism by opponents of special privilege, such attacks did not reach a climax until the 1830s and 1840s. By then, however, corporate law had been sufficiently privatized to make the corporation, whether new or old, virtually impervious to political challenge. The *Dartmouth College* case had made that certain. Chancellor James Kent, the author of the single most influential treatise on American law in the nineteenth century, commented that *Dartmouth College* "did more than any other single act, proceeding from the authority of the United States, to throw an impregnable barrier around all rights and franchises derived from the grant of government; and to give solidity and inviolability to the literary, charitable, religious and commercial institutions of our country."[43] For Kent *Dartmouth College* was a great decision. But Ichabod Bartlett, attorney for the state of New Hampshire in the *Dartmouth College* litigation, concluded that "the government must control these institutions [the corporations] or they shall control the government!"[44]

Labor Law

The growth of the private corporation notwithstanding, the notion persisted that some organizations were of such profound public concern that they should remain within the control of the public law. Early labor unions fell into this category. In the eyes of the law they were "criminal conspiracies." Indeed, at the very time when the corporate form as a legal entity was breaking away from public control, American courts established the doctrine that labor associations were conspiracies in restraint of trade—a doctrine of labor law that remained virtually unbroken until 1842.[45]

In the late eighteenth century, journeymen cordwainers (shoemakers) in eastern cities organized for the purpose of establishing minimum rates of pay. They attempted to set up what would later be called the "closed shop"—closed, that is, to nonassociating workers. When master craftsmen tried to hire "nonunion" journeymen, the cordwainers struck. In retaliation, the masters organized their own associations and proceeded to initiate prosecutions against the or-

---

[43] James Kent, *Commentaries on American Law* (5th ed., New York, 1844), vol. I, p. 418.
[44] Quoted in Charles G. Haines, *The Role of the Supreme Court in American Government and Politics, 1789–1835* (New York, 1960), p. 416.
[45] *Commonwealth v. Hunt,* 45 Mass. (4 Metc.) 111 (1842).

ganized journeymen for criminal conspiracy. This was the beginning of what would be a major trend in American labor history—use of the courts and of the legal process by employers to curb union activity. In the case of the cordwainers, the heavy hand of the criminal law was employed successfully to destroy voluntary associative activity by working people.[46]

The issues that came to a head in the Cordwainer cases were central questions of American law. Despite the fact that this was a period when the English common law was under attack in America, the common law of criminal conspiracy—the most shadowy and oppressive part of the entire body of the English criminal law—was applied to labor unions and put into effect in many American jurisdictions.[47] The problem of jury bias also surfaced in these cases. In the 1806 Philadelphia case, for example, of the twelve members of the jury that convicted members of the Federal Society of Journeymen Cordwainers, nine were merchants and three were master craftsmen—hardly a balanced panel to decide whether journeymen could organize.[48] In the Cordwainer cases the courts held that labor combinations were illegal conspiracies if the *purpose* of the combination, such as to raise wages, or the *means* employed, such as calling a strike, were illegal. Unions that coerced nonunion journeymen or master craftsmen with strikes, or other actions "in restraint of trade" that were prejudicial to the public, easily satisfied either the "illegal purpose" test or the "illegal means" test. For all practical purposes, any activity undertaken by a journeymen's union was bound to result in criminal indictment and conviction under these legal doctrines.

What is most interesting from a broad historical perspective, however, is the comparison between the posture of the law toward early trade unionists and its posture toward the process of business incorporation. What cries out for comment is the obvious double standard. While private incorporators, in furthering their own economic interests, could limit their civil liability under the new law of incorporation, journeymen craftsmen invited criminal sanctions by associating together for a similar purpose. Moreover, the law imposed no liability, criminal or

[46] John R. Commons, et al., *History of Labour in the United States*, 4 vols. (New York, 1966), vol. 1, chap 5.
[47] The issue reinforced political divisions between the Jeffersonians, who in principle opposed the wholesale application of English legal rules to America, and the Federalists, who generally were in favor of the "reception" of English law.
[48] Commons, *History of Labour*, vol. 1, p. 147.

civil, on associations by master craftsmen. Thus the law permitted employers to organize to fight their employees, but it prohibited employees from organizing in their own self-interest to fight their bosses.

Indeed, while the right to associate freely was generally recognized in almost every important sphere of life, noneconomic as well as economic, associations of wage earners were singled out for special attention and control. As defense counsel in the Philadelphia Cordwainer case argued:

> Shall all others, except only the industrious mechanics be allowed to meet and plot; merchants to determine their prices current, or settle the markets, politicians to electioneer, sportsmen for horse-racing and games, ladies and gentlemen for balls, parties and [banquets]; and yet these poor men be indicted for combining against starvation?[49]

Political, religious, and social associations of all kinds were perfectly legal. Political parties and religious sects, once the targets of criminal prosecution, were now legitimate. Even some economic associations—private incorporating investors and unions of master craftsmen—were acceptable. But working people who sold their labor for wages still felt the sting and punishment of public law despite constitutional provisions protecting the "right in a peaceable manner to assemble together for the common good."[50] Clearly, powerful class bias was at work. This is particularly evident in view of the jury selection process, which, as exemplified by the Philadelphia Cordwainer case, was so heavily weighted in favor of the master craftsman. Thus, at the same time that the law was in the process of releasing the business corporation from political control by transforming it from a public law to a private law entity, under the Cordwainer decisions early trade unions became ever more vulnerable to criminal prosecution.

There are still other ways to understand the Cordwainer cases. On the surface, they appear to be truly exceptional to the general trend of privatization. But on a deeper level, the anomalies of these early labor cases can be reconciled with that pervasive theme. In the limited-liability private corporation cases, as in the Cordwainer cases, the courts put much emphasis on the issue of coercion. In the sphere of corporation law, neither the corporation itself nor its creditors could assess the

---

[49] Quoted in ibid., p. 141. See also Document 18.
[50] Pennsylvania Constitution (1790), Art. IX, Sec. 20.

personal assets of shareholders beyond what shareholders had assented to by contract. And under the Cordwainer decisions journeymen could not force union membership on recalcitrant craftsmen. In the New York Cordwainer case, for example, the union had secured the discharge from employment of a member who had not paid his dues, and for this reason the New York court found that the methods used by the cordwainers were illegal. The ideology underlying these decisions was freedom from restraint. But the encouragement of labor mobility ran parallel to the argument that commercial expansion was best served by the free movement of investment capital. Just as monopoly and special privilege placed unwanted restraints on capital resources, so the economic restraints imposed by labor unions disrupted the workings of Adam Smith's "invisible hand." In both instances, the stress was on individualism, voluntary association, and noncoercion—the same themes animating other zones of law in the postrevolutionary period.

The Cordwainer cases illustrate the ways in which the transition from public law to private law was arrested in the labor market, where society preferred to retain firm control because of deep fears about working-class power. These fears have persisted. The special posture of the law toward employer-employee relations has had a continuing history in America. Long after the collapse of the labor conspiracy doctrine, antitrust legislation, fashioned to curb the excesses of industrial combinations in the late nineteenth century, was turned against industrial unions. The failure of the journeymen cordwainers in the prosecutions brought against them in the early years of the nineteenth century must have convinced many working people that the legal-constitutional system was a system built for the wealthy and the powerful, not for the indigent and the politically weak.

4

The Legal Profession

Why did the deep changes in American law outlined above occur in the period after the American Revolution? What social forces generated these radical shifts in direction away from public law values toward private law? In short, why was the public estate diminished in so many areas by the advance of the private law? Clearly, one answer is that the legal profession's special orientation to American society had much to do with this legal transformation. The recruitment, education, and socialization of lawyers into the legal profession, and the emergence of that profession as a powerful and independent force in American life, supplied the basic underpinnings for substantive legal change.

In the period after the American Revolution there was a sudden increase of lawyers—not merely in absolute numbers but relative to population growth itself. One social historian has estimated that from 1783 to 1820 the number of lawyers grew four times faster than the general population, which itself was expanding at an enormous rate because of natural increase and immigration.[1] The figures in Table 3 give some indication of that increase.

The statistics for Massachusetts are particularly interesting because they show that while there was a net decrease in the number of lawyers as a result of Tory emigration during and immediately after the American Revolution, the rapid growth of the legal profession that had taken place in that state in the late colonial period had resumed by the mid-

---

[1] David Hackett Fischer, "The Legal System" (NEH seminar paper, Brandeis University, 1979), pp. 10–41. By permission.

Table 3

Number of Lawyers in Three Selected States, to 1820

	Number of Lawyers	**Lawyers per 10,000 population**
		Massachusetts (including Maine)
1740	15	10
1775	71	24
1780	34	11
1785	92	24
1790	112	24
1800	200	35
1810	492	70
1820	710	87
		Connecticut
1790	129	54
1800	169	67
1820	248	90
		South Carolina
1771	24	19
1820	200	40

Source: David H. Fischer, "The Legal System"; Gerard W. Gawalt, *The Promise of Power: The Emergence of the Legal Profession in Massachusetts, 1760–1840* (Westport, Conn., 1979), p. 14.

1780s. How were these new lawyers trained? What were the larger consequences of that training to the growth and shape of American law?

Legal education in the early years of American history was quite different from what it was to become in the nineteenth and twentieth centuries. In the colonial period, most lawyers who trained in America rather than at the English Inns of Court[2] worked as apprentices in the law offices of established professionals. Each master practitioner defined the tasks and the education of his apprentice-clerks differently, and the amount of time served varied greatly. Law clerks usually spent

---

[2] The Inns of Court in London, "little more than living and eating clubs" by the eighteenth century, were near the central common-law courts. Students read law and observed trials while living at the Inns. See Lawrence M. Friedman, *A History of American Law* (New York. 1973), p. 84.

most of their working hours copying forms, drafting pleadings and briefs, and doing whatever office chores the master required. The oral instruction the novice received was entirely within the control of his teacher, and most of the time the practitioner was too busy to give much attention to his clerk. The chief benefit the student received was the experience of working in a law office, ready access to the published books or manuscript folios in the office library, and personal contact with lawyers, clients, and the legal process.

For such privileges, students or their families paid handsome fees— as in the case of one famous general who paid tuition so that his nephew, a future Supreme Court justice, could study law:

> Phila. March 22, 1782. I promise to pay James Wilson Esq. or order on demand one hundred guineas, his fee for receiving my nephew Bushrod Washington as a student of law in his office.
>
> G. Washington.[3]

Bushrod Washington's teacher, James Wilson, went on to become an associate justice of the United States Supreme Court. He was also one of the great legal and political thinkers of his day. But Wilson was not, apparently, a great law teacher. Another contemporary reported that

> as an instructor he was almost useless to those who were under his direction. He would never engage with them in professional discussion; to a direct question he gave the shortest possible answer and a general request for information was always refused.[4]

The reminiscences of early American lawyers reflecting on their days as law office clerks are replete with such complaints about the neglect, boredom, and tedium of the life of a law student. William Livingston of New York, for example, who in 1745 was a student of James Alexander, one of the leading colonial attorneys of the time, wrote to a New York newspaper to complain about his teacher:

> [I]f [lawyers] deserve the imputation of injustice and dishonesty, it is in no instance more visible and notorious, then in their conduct towards their apprentices.[5]

---

[3] Quoted in Charles Warren, *A History of the American Bar* (Boston, 1911), p. 166.
[4] Quoted in *ibid.,* p. 167.
[5] Quoted in *ibid.*

Livingston called his teacher's conduct "scandalous, horrid, base, and infamous to the last degree."

The great Justice Joseph Story suffered as a student. Left alone by his law teacher to fathom the depths of *Coke on Littleton,* a standard English lawbook, Story reported later that he "took it up, and after trying it day after day with very little success, I sat myself down and wept bitterly. My tears dropped upon the book, and stained its pages."[6]

Some students were more fortunate. John Quincy Adams was lucky enough to have Theophilus Parsons, later chief justice of the Massachusetts Supreme Judicial Court, as his teacher:

> Nov. 27, 1787. It is of great advantage to us to have Mr. Parsons in the office. He is in himself a law library, and proficient in every useful branch of service; but his chief excellency is, that no student can be more fond of proposing questions than he is of solving them. He is never at a loss, and always gives a full and ample account, not only of the subject proposed, but of all matters which have any intimate connection with it. I am persuaded that the advantage of having such an instructor is very great, and I hope I shall not misimprove [*sic*] it as some of his pupils have done.[7]

The first American law schools were outgrowths of this law office apprenticeship system. Practitioners who were better at teaching than they were in representing clients began to attract a student following. Their offices expanded as the numbers of their students grew. Table 4 lists the private law schools of this expanded apprenticeship model founded in this period. Some lasted well into the nineteenth century. The most famous of these was the Litchfield Law School established by Tapping Reeve in 1784 in Litchfield, Connecticut. In the half-century of its existence, Litchfield produced over one thousand graduates.[8] Students came from all over the country to attend the law lectures given there. The Litchfield Law School was not only one of the earliest law schools in the country; it was also the first law school of national reputation. Many of its graduates became famous lawyers and judges. Three among them, Levi Woodbury of New Hampshire, Henry Baldwin of Pennsylvania, and Ward Hunt of New York were appointed associate justices of the United States Supreme Court. Two other Litchfield

---

[6] Quoted in Albert J. Harno, *Legal Education in the United States* (San Francisco, 1953), p. 20.
[7] Quoted in Warren, *History of the American Bar,* p. 169.
[8] Samuel H. Fisher, *Litchfield Law School, 1774–1833: Biographical Catalogue of Students,* Yale Law Library Publications, No. 11 (May, 1946).

52   *Law in the New Republic*

Table 4
Private Law Schools Before 1835, by State

Name of Law School	Location	Date Founded (if known)	Date Closed (if known)
Virginia			
Wythe's Law School	Williamsburg	1779	1791
Wythe's Law School	Richmond	1791	c.1806
Taylor's Law School	Needham	1821	——
St. George Tucker's Law School	Winchester	1824	1830
Lomax's Law School	Fredericksburg	1830	——
Connecticut			
Litchfield Law School	Litchfield	1784	1833
Staple's Law School	New Haven	1800	1824
Gilbert's Law School	Hebron	1810	1816
Swift's Law School	Windham	——	——
New York			
Van Schaak's Law School	Kinderhook	1786	1828
New York Law Institute	——	1826	——
Kentucky			
Transylvania Law School	Lexington	1799	1861
Tennessee			
Powell's Law School	Blountville	c.1800	——
Haywood's Law School	Nashville	1807	——
Vermont			
Turner's Law School	Fairfield	1806	1812
Massachusetts			
Howe's Law School	Northampton	1823	1829
Metcalf's Law School	Dedham	1828	c.1829
Pennsylvania			
Dickinson's Law Academy	Philadelphia	1821	——
Maryland			
Dorsey's Law School	Baltimore	——	1823

Adapted from Fischer, "The Legal System," pp. 10–44. See also Alfred Z. Reed, *Training for the Public Profession of the Law* (New York, 1921), app. B.

graduates, John C. Calhoun of South Carolina and Aaron Burr of New York, later achieved political stature (and in Burr's case, subsequent disgrace) as Vice Presidents of the United States. Still others became prominent in business, journalism, and education.

Teaching at Litchfield was by the lecture method. Extant student notebooks and teacher memoranda reveal the subject matter covered in these lectures, most of which were given by Judge Reeve and his close associate, Judge James Gould. These teachers concentrated on the major fields of private law and gave scant notice to the main areas of public law. In one Litchfield course, for example, 26 pages of lecture notes were devoted to "municipal law" (the law of government) and 87 pages were devoted to "public wrongs or criminal law." But the lectures on "private wrongs or torts" required 60 pages, "contracts" required 97 pages, "bailments" required 129 pages, "bills of exchange and promissory notes" required 73 pages, and "mercantile law" required 167 pages.[9] Clearly, courses on private law subjects received extensive treatment at Litchfield whereas attention to public law was minimal.

In contrast with Litchfield's narrow and technical definition of the elements of legal training, however, was the broader conceptual approach taken by David Hoffman of Maryland. Hoffman published his *Course of Legal Study* in 1817, in preparing for the law lectureship at the new University of Maryland. His book on legal education is an extraordinary contrast with the training available at Litchfield. In it Hoffman, himself a leading member of the Maryland bar, made an attempt to open the mind of the student to a large universe of learning peopled by ancients as well as moderns; philosophers, theologians, historians, and statesmen as well as lawyers and jurists.

Five of the thirteen "titles" of Hoffman's book were devoted to public law subjects: The Elementary and Constitutional Principles of the Municipal Law of England, of the United States, and of the Roman or Civil Law (Title II), The Law of Crimes and Punishments (Title VII), The Law of Nations (Title VIII), The Constitution and Laws of the United States (Title XI), and The Constitution and Laws of the Several States of the Union (Title XII). Three further titles were Moral and Political Philosophy (Title I), the Civil or Roman Law (Title X), and Political Economy (Title XIII). The remaining five titles, less than half of the total, dealt with subjects that generally would fall within the private or commercial law sphere: The Law of Real Rights and Real Remedies (Title III), The Law of Personal Rights and Personal

[9] Samuel H. Fisher, "The Litchfield Law School," Connecticut Tercentenary Commission, Committee on Historical Publications, pp. 6–8; reprinted in Henry L. Shepherd (ed.), *Litchfield: Portrait of a Beautiful Town* (1969), at pp. 40–62. I am grateful to Mr. Charles C. Goetsch of New Haven for alerting me to Samuel H. Fisher's articles on Litchfield. Mr. Goetsch is editing the student lecture notes from Litchfield Law School for publication. His research promises to have a significant impact on early American legal history.

Remedies (Title IV), the Lex Mercatoria or Merchant's Law (Title VI), and Maritime and Admiralty Law (Title IX).

Hoffman captured the spirit of his work in his introduction to the book:

> He who aspires to a thorough acquaintance with legal science, should cultivate the most enlarged ideas of its transcendent dignity, its vital importance, its boundless extent, and infinite variety. As it relates to the conduct of man, it is a moral science of great sublimity; as its object is individual and national happiness, it is, of all others, the most important; as it respects the moral actions of men, and of nations, it is infinitely varied; and as it concerns all his rights and obligations, either derived from, or due to his God, his neighbour, his country, or himself, it must necessarily be a science of vast extent.[10]

In short, David Hoffman conceived of the law as a "liberal" profession. Its study and practice would broaden the mind and uplift the spirit.[11]

Hoffman's *Course of Legal Study* influenced curriculum development at Harvard Law School, founded in 1817, and at the University of Virginia Law School, founded in 1826. At Columbia University, law lectures were given by James Kent in 1794 and 1795 and then again in the mid-1820s. Kent published his lectures in his great four-volume treatise, *Commentaries on American Law*.[12] Like Hoffman's *Course of Legal Study,* the *Commentaries* contained a much higher public law content than anything offered at Litchfield. The entire first volume of the work, one-fourth of the whole, was devoted to the law of nations, American constitutional law, and the sources of municipal law in the several states. While the *Commentaries* lacked the broad philosophical and historical orientation of Hoffman's book, it did contain numerous references to ancient law and to European civil law. James Kent, himself the Chancellor of New York, was widely read and thoroughly educated, and his influential book, which went through numerous editions in the nineteenth century, was the product of his liberal education.

But despite its narrow technicalism, perhaps because of it, Litchfield was unquestionably the most influential national law school in America prior to the emergence of the law schools with academic affiliations such

---

[10] David Hoffman, *A Course of Legal Study,* 2nd ed. (Baltimore, 1836), p. 23.
[11] Perry Miller (ed.), *The Legal Mind in America: From Independence to the Civil War* (Garden City, N.Y., 1962), p. 84.
[12] James Kent, *Commentaries on American Law,* 4 vols. (1826–1830).

as Harvard, Columbia, and the University of Virginia. In the period of its professional dominance, Litchfield emphasized the practitioner's arts rather than philosophical education. This meant that leading lawyers from every state spent the formative years of their professional development in an intellectual environment in which technical competence in the fields of private law was valued much more highly than learning in public law subjects. The training that great numbers of lawyers received, in law offices and in apprentice-model schools of the Litchfield type, stressed mastery of those skills most highly prized by private litigants. The teaching, although intensive and sometimes masterful, lacked a broad humanistic base.

Thus legal training and general education remained separate and distinct. This divorce between professional training and general education was best exemplified by the institutional detachment of schools such as Litchfield from the leading colleges of the day. Indeed, even when the academic law schools replaced the private academies and became the main centers of legal education, they were run and taught by practitioners. Like the medical schools and the other vocational satellites of the early universities, the academic law schools were not really organically connected to the liberal arts colleges and universities of which they were a part. This has remained a dominant characteristic of American law schools. Unlike European law schools, where law teaching is more integrated into the general curriculum, American law schools still maintain a detachment and distance from the main life of the university, although in the twentieth century this situation has been mitigated somewhat by the emergence of a regular law professoriat with full-time teaching and academic commitments.

The practitioners and former practitioners who taught at Litchfield, at other private law schools, and at the early academic centers of legal education had virtually no opportunity to develop a wider vision of the role of law in the achievement of broad social purposes. Preoccupation with mastery of the technical arts of legal practice meant that the strictures that David Hoffman had enumerated in his introduction to *A Course of Legal Study* had little meaning for a large proportion of the first several generations of postrevolutionary American lawyers. As Hoffman wrote in the preface to the second edition of his book: "The prejudices of early education adhere... with wonderful tenacity."[13] Those prejudices helped to determine not only the values that the legal

[13] Hoffman, *Course of Legal Study*, p. ix.

profession continued to consider of preeminent importance but the substance of the law they practiced and of the legal system they did so much to shape.

The spirit of school law taught in institutions such as Litchfield was pervasive because of the enormous influence of lawyers in American society. Lawyers occupied key positions in government and were achieving increasing importance in the emerging corporate bureaucracies. To be sure there were divisions within the profession between frontier lawyers and the urban bar, between untrained "pettifoggers" and the products of the schools, between those who represented the poor and the "middling" classes and those associated with the rich and the well-born. Such divisions explain much about antilawyer sentiment and the battles fought over professional standards, bar admission procedures, and methods of judicial selection.[14] But historical attention to divisions within the legal profession has slighted the great importance of the profession as a brotherhood with common interests sharing a single universe of discourse.

No one understood this better than Alexis De Tocqueville. After an extensive journey through the United States in the early 1830s, which he undertook in order to examine American prisons,[15] De Tocqueville wrote what has become the classic study of American democracy. The young French aristocrat viewed the legal profession as a separate rank within American society. According to De Tocqueville, lawyers "naturally constitute *a body;* not by any previous understanding, or by an agreement that directs them to a common end; but the analogy of their studies and the uniformity of their methods connect their minds as a common interest might unite their endeavors."[16]

In the absence of a native aristocracy, and in a nation where "the people" were sovereign, lawyers occupied a mediating position between the democratic majority and the governing elite. Committed to the preservation of the legal order, which they controlled, the legal profession provided a natural counterpoise to the radical inclinations of

[14] Maxwell Bloomfield, *American Lawyers in a Changing Society, 1776-1876* (Cambridge, Mass., 1976), chaps. 2, 5; Alfred Z. Reed, *Training for the Public Profession of the Law* (New York, 1921), part II, passim.

[15] The best treatment of the history of the American prison reform movement in the nineteenth century is David J. Rothman, *The Discovery of the Asylum: Social Order and Disorder in the New Republic* (Boston, 1971), chaps. 3-4.

[16] Alexis De Tocqueville, *Democracy in America,* Phillips Bradley, (ed.), 2 vols. (New York, 1944), vol. I, p. 283.

the popular will. One result of this restraint was the absence of innovation in private law in comparison with the radical transformation in public law which the revolution had brought about. As De Tocqueville put it, "The Americans, who have made so many innovations in their political laws, have introduced very sparing alterations in their civil laws, and that with great difficulty, although many of these laws are repugnant to their social condition. The reason for this is that in matters of civil law the majority are obliged to defer to the authority of the legal profession, and the American lawyers are disinclined to innovate when they are left to their own choice."[17] De Tocqueville likened the lawyers to the "hierophants of Egypt," keepers of "an occult science," who by profession rather than by birth harbored aristocratic pretensions. The profession "secretly opposed [its] aristocratic propensities to the nation's democratic instincts, their superstitious attachment to what is old to [the people's] love of novelty, their narrow views to its immense designs and their habitual procrastination to its ardent impatience."[18]

The power of the legal profession as a cohesive force in American life was strengthened by the joinder of the bench and the bar. Lay advocacy disappeared in most states after the revolution. In addition, the colonial practice of elevating laypersons as well as lawyers to the highest courts in some of the colonies came to an end in most states.[19] These developments meant that the bar would become thoroughly professionalized and the bench would be drawn from its ranks. Thereafter, judges and lawyers would emanate from the same pool of training and experience. Furthermore, the courts wrested control over bar admission requirements from county bar associations, thereby increasing the fusion of bench and bar and weakening even more the independence of the lawyers from the courts.[20]

The growth of judicial independence reinforced these tendencies. The Constitution recognized the principle of an independent judiciary when it provided that federal judges would have permanent tenure in office and could be removed only for extraordinary causes. Once appointed by the president, federal judges could not be removed except by impeachment, a device rarely used. While most of the states adopted the elective principle rather than appointment as a method of judicial

[17] Ibid., p. 290.
[18] Ibid., p. 289.
[19] Lawrence M. Friedman, *A History of American Law* (New York, 1973), pp. 109-110.
[20] Ibid., p. 276; Reed, *Public Profession of the Law*, part II.

selection, judicial office was usually not contested in the same way as other elective positions. The state judiciaries became non-political—at least with respect to recruitment to the bench. Thus, both the federal and the state judiciaries, in different ways, became independent of day-to-day politics. This independence was a source of great influence. "The courts of justice are the visible organs by which the legal profession is enabled to control the democracy," De Tocqueville observed.[21] Clearly the legal profession, the judges together with the lawyers, had become a force with unmatched social leverage and power.

But the extraordinary power of the legal profession in American life was the result not only of the peculiar legal, constitutional, and political framework of American society and the fusion of the bench and the bar into a cohesive force. Of equal importance was the enormous deference the American people began to give to legal professionals and the degree to which the American public absorbed the ideas and the habits of mind of the legal profession. The very language of the lawyers became what De Tocqueville called the "vulgar tongue" of public life.

Several forces combined to make it so. Because lawyers played such a prominent role in politics and occupied a disproportionate number of public offices, political issues of great consequence were often distilled into erudite legal questions, and political positions were defined as doctrines or propositions of law. Thus the greatest public issue of the nineteenth century, black slavery, the issue over which the nation was to break apart in 1860, was addressed not in moral terms or in terms of social cost but primarily as a series of technical problems of constitutional law—particularly, whether or not Congress had the power to exclude slavery in the territories, a place occupied by very few masters and slaves by the outbreak of the Civil War.

De Tocqueville attributed this penetration of the social fabric by the legal mentality to the jury system. "The jury," he wrote, "is preeminently a political institution. . . ."[22] The civil jury especially "cannot fail to exercise a powerful influence upon the national character."[23] De Tocqueville had a very positive view of the jury system and its effects. He found that jury service was as widespread as the franchise and about as frequently exercised. This exposure to the judicial process imparted a sense of equity, social responsibility, and participation in self-govern-

---

[21] De Tocqueville, *Democracy in America,* vol. I, p. 289.
[22] Ibid., p. 294.
[23] Ibid., p. 295.

ment to the citizen. De Tocqueville also thought that jury service was a highly educative experience, teaching both a rudimentary knowledge of the law and its application to actual cases. Jury service transmitted to the citizenry the spirit of the judges, whose influence upon the jury panel was almost unlimited. Their influence, in fact, extended "far beyond the limits of the courts; in the recreations of private life, as well as in the turmoil of public business, in public, and in the legislative assemblies, the American judge is constantly surrounded by men who are accustomed to regard his intelligence as superior to their own; and after having exercised his power in the decision of causes, he continues to influence the habits of thought, and even the characters, of those who acted with him in his official capacity."[24]

The justification for the jury in a system of constitutional democracy has always been that it represents a check upon the power of the judges through citizen participation in the execution of the laws.[25] But De Tocqueville showed that the contact between judge and jury worked both ways. The deference of the typical jury to the judge's instructions on the law, and the judge's abiding influence on the mind of the jurors even after the trial ended, exposed a fundamental truth. De Tocqueville put it best: "The jury, then which seems to restrict the rights of the judiciary, does in reality consolidate its power; and in no country are the judges so powerful as where the people share their privileges. It is especially by means of the jury in civil causes that the American magistrates imbue even the lower classes of society with the spirit of their profession."[26]

Thus the shift in emphasis from public law to private law in the period after the revolution was a result not only of the pivotal role of the legal profession in public life, but also of the power the legal profession exercised over the American mind.

[24] Ibid., p. 297.
[25] By 1820 a clear functional differentiation between the role of the judge and the jury had come about. The jury was the finder of *fact* and the judge the definer of *law*. See Friedman, *History of American Law*, p. 137.
[26] De Tocqueville, *Democracy in America*, vol. I, p. 297.

II. Documents

Introduction

The documentary section which follows is divided into two parts. The first consists of a broad selection of documents which have been referred to in the text. The materials chosen include legal cases, constitutional provisions, statutes and other sources. Each document is preceded by a short introduction which gives basic historical background so that the document can be read in a meaningful context. In addition, the introductions pose questions which should be considered while the document is read and which may provide starting points for group discussion. Each introduction also lists a convenient published collection where the document can be read in its entirety if the whole has not been reprinted here. Finally, the introduction provides a secondary source reference for further reading.

The second part consists of a group of documents related to the New Orleans Batture land controversy of the early nineteenth century. A general introduction to this section provides the reader with sufficient contextual background so that separate introductions are not required for each document. Indeed, the absence of annotations offers the student the opportunity to read each document with a fresh perspective.

1. Concord Resolutions (1776)* ════════

On September 17, 1776, the Massachusetts House of Representatives proposed to the "male inhabitants of each town" that the Massachusetts legislature draft a constitution for the state of Massachusetts-Bay. The resolutions of Concord, passed on October 22, 1776, represent the answer of one town meeting to this proposal. The Concord "return" shows a clear understanding that a written constitution and a legislative statute are two very different kinds of enacted laws. A constitution codifies "fundamental law," whereas a statute is a mere formulation of "ordinary law." On the basis of this understanding, Concord resolved that the political forum needed for the adoption of one was not appropriate for the other. What reasons are given for drawing this institutional distinction? Why did Concord insist that each Massachusetts town, regardless of size, be guaranteed at least one delegate to the proposed convention? Would this not lead to the over-representation of people in the smallest towns as compared to those who lived in larger towns? How could this apparent departure from pure popular representation be justified?

At a meeting of the Inhabitents of the Town of Concord being free & twenty one years of age and upwards, met by adjournment on the twenty first Day of October 1776 to take into Consideration a Resolve of the Honorable House of Representatives of this State on the 17th of September Last the Town Resolved as followes—

Resolve 1st: That this State being at Present destitute of a Properly established form of Government, it is absolutely necessary that one should be immediatly formed and established—

Resolved 2: That the Supreme Legislative, either in their Proper Capacity, or in Joint Committee, are by no means a Body proper to form & Establish a Constitution, or form of Government; for Reasons following. First Because we Conceive that a Constitution in its Proper Idea intends a System of Principles Established to Secure the Subject in the Possession & enjoyment of their Rights & Privileges, against any Encroachments of the Governing Part—2d Because the Same Body that forms a Constitution have of Consequence a power to alter it. 3d— Because a Constitution alterable by the Supreme Legislative is no

---

* Source: Massachusetts (State) Archives, vol. 156, p. 167. Available in Robert J. Taylor (ed.), *Massachusetts, Colony to Commonwealth: Documents on the Formation of its Constitution, 1775–1780* (New York, 1972), pp. 45–46.

For further reading: Oscar and Mary Handlin (eds.), *The Popular Sources of Political Authority: Documents on the Massachusetts Constitution of 1780* (Cambridge, Mass., 1966), pp. 1–54.

Security at all to the Subject against any Encroachment of the Governing part on any or on all of their Rights and priviliges.

Resolved 3d. That it appears to this Town highly necessary & Expedient that a Convention, or Congress be immediatly Chosen, to form & establish a Constitution, by the Inhabitants of the Respective Towns in this State, being free & of twenty one years of age, and upwards, in Proportion as the Representatives of this State formerly were Chosen; the Convention or Congress not to Consist of a greater number then the House of assembly of this State heretofore might Consist of, Except that each Town & District Shall have the Liberty to Send one Representative, or otherwise as Shall appear meet to the Inhabitents of this State in General.

Resolve 4th. that when the Convention, or Congress have formed a Constitution they adjourn for a Short time, and Publish their Proposed Constitution for the Inspection and Remarks of the Inhabitents of this State.

Resolved 5ly. that the Honorable House of assembly of this State be Desired to Recommend it to the Inhabitents of the State to Proceed to Chuse a Convention or Congress for the Purpas abovesaid as soon as Possable.

A True Copy of the Proceeding of the Town of Concord at the General Town meeting above mentioned—attest Ephraim Wood, Jr., Town Clerk

2. Philadelphia Broadside (1776)*

Since a written constitution codified the fundamental law of the polity, to which all other law was subsidiary, elections to the body that would draft the constitution were of paramount importance. The campaign broadside of the Philadelphia Committee of Correspondence illustrates the significance of the state constitutional convention to Pennsylvanians. The broadside also reflects the view, widely held in the eighteenth century, that political responsibility ought to be bestowed only on men (not women) and that these men should be "disinterested"—that is, they should "have no interest besides the common

* Available in Clifford R. Shipton (ed.), *Early American Imprints, 1639-1800: A Readex Microprint of the Works Listed in Evans' American Bibliography* (Worcester, Mass., 1962-1968), no. 15115.

For further reading: Eric Foner, *Thomas Paine and Revolutionary America* (New York, 1976), chap. 4.

*Interest of Mankind." Such men, contemporaries believed, were motivated by
"virtue" rather than by motives of self-interest. A sure sign of impure motivation
and self-aggrandizement was active solicitation of political support. Nevertheless, despite its strictures about "the common good," the broadside is not a
politically neutral document. In fact it expresses some of the most salient
elements of the "radical" position on the constitution-making process. Can you
identify the elements of that "radicalism"? How do you explain what appears to
be a fundamental inconsistency between the call for disinterestedness on the one
hand and the identification of particular ideological tests for political prefer-
ment on the other?*

TO THE SEVERAL BATTALIONS OF MILITARY ASSOCIATORS IN THE PROVINCE OF PENNSYLVANIA, JUNE 26, 1776

The Committee of Privates of the City and Liberties of Philadelphia would esteem itself culpable, if it neglected to address you on the most important Subject that can come before Freemen — You are about to hold an Election on the Eighth of next Month; and on the Judiciousness of the Choice which you then make, depends the Happiness of Millions of unborn — The Excellence or Defectiveness of a Constitution which must last for Ages, hangs on the Choice of the Day — and, remember, the Complexion of your Government, and the State of your future Laws, will spring from the Constitution: You ought, therefore, to chuse such Men as are most equal to the Task — Permit us then to point out to you the Qualifications which we think most essential to constitute a member of the approaching Convention — A Government made for the common Good should be framed by Men who can have no interest besides the common Interest of Mankind. It is the Happiness of America that there is no Rank above that of Freeman existing in it; and much of our future Welfare and Tranquility will depend on its remaining so forever; for this Reason, great and over-grown rich Men will be improper to be trusted, they will be too apt to be framing Distinctions in Society, because they will reap the Benefits of all such Distinctions — Gentlemen of the learned Professions are generally filled with Quirks and Quibbles of the Schools; and, though we have several worthy Men of great Learning among us, yet, as they are very apt to indulge their Disposition to Refinement to a culpable Degree, we would think it prudent not to have too great a Proportion of such in the Convention—Honesty, common sense, and a plain Understanding, when unbiased by sinister Motives, are fully equal to the Task — Men of like Passions and Interests with ourselves are the most likely to frame us a good Constitution — You will, upon this Occasion, no doubt, find Men of otherwise suspicious Characters strive, by every Art in their Power to recommend themselves to your Favour — But, remember, the Man who is at any Time solicitous to be employed by you as your Representative, is rarely the most worthy of your Confidence, and at this Time it is sufficient to reprobate him in the Judgment of wise Men — For, be assured, that though Honesty and plain Understanding may be equal to the Task, few Men will ardently long after it who have nothing but your Interest in View.... Would it not be prudent to instruct your Deputies, when chosen to reserve an Annual Return of all Power into your Hand. No Officer of Government should hold his Commission but by the free Voice of the People, annually expressed — Officers of the Militia should be chosen by the Militia — the Officers of the regular Army, when necessary, by the Legislature. — Legislators and Executors of Law by the Freemen of the District where they reside, whom they represent, and for whose sake they exist. — Trust no Man but such who is determined to extend the Principle of a free Annual Election, by Ballot, to all possible Cases; for in the constant Exercise of this Principle alone consists the soul of Freedom. — He who would incline to restrain it in any Case whatever, where it can be conveniently exercised, loves not Liberty — No Man will extend it far enough, who can find it his Interest to do otherwise. — You will have an Aristocracy, or Government of the Great, if improper Persons are to form your Constitution. Let no Power have any Hand in framing your Laws, but one, and let that one be your immediate Representatives in General Assembly, annually, chosen by Ballot — You will then have no Negative put upon good Laws, nor Refusal to repeal bad ones. — Let no Man ever hold a Place in the Legislature, and be an Executor of the Laws at the same Time. — Keep the Legislative and Executive Authority for ever separate — The Man who would not provide a Principle in the Constitution for keeping them apart, should never have a Hand in framing the Constitution — Your own good Sense will point out the Characters, from which there can be no Danger. Chuse them, and oblige Mankind and your humble Servants.

3. Pennsylvania Constitution (1776)*

Many Americans considered the Pennsylvania Constitution of 1776 to be the most radical state constitution of the revolutionary era. They believed that the volatility of Pennsylvania politics was directly attributable to the constitutional structure of Pennsylvania's government. Indeed, one of the important reasons why the framers of the U.S. Constitution decided to locate the permanent seat of the federal government in a separate federal enclave, and not in Philadelphia, was because of a pervasive fear that Philadelphia was too prone to political violence. The elements of Pennsylvania's constitutional radicalism are fairly obvious: (1) a unicameral legislature, (2) replacement of the governor with a president and council, (3) liberalized voting and officeholding requirements, and (4) provision for frequent constitutional amendment. Note that section 2 refers to "legislative power" and section 3 to "executive power"; but section 4 speaks of "courts of justice" rather than of "judicial power." Why was this terminology employed? Which provisions of the constitution recognize a clear separation of powers principle? Are there any elements of the Pennsylvania constitution that might have been considered conservative? What advantages and dangers beset the process of constitutional review set forth in section 47?

Section 1. The commonwealth or state of Pennsylvania shall be governed hereafter by an assembly of the representatives of the freemen of the same, and a president and council, in manner and form following—

Sect. 2. The supreme legislative power shall be vested in a house of representatives of the freemen of the commonwealth or state of Pennsylvania.

Sect. 3. The supreme executive power shall be vested in a president and council.

Sect. 4. Courts of justice shall be established in the city of Philadelphia, and in every country of this state.

Sect. 5. The freemen of this commonwealth and their sons shall be trained and armed for its defence under such regulations, restrictions, and exceptions as the general assembly shall by law direct, preserving always to the people the right of choosing their colonel and all commissioned officers under that rank, in such manner and as often as by the said laws shall be directed.

* Plan or Frame of Government for the Commonwealth or State of Pennsylvania. Available in Francis N. Thorpe (ed.), *The Federal and State Constitutions* (Washington, D.C., 1909), vol. 5.

For further reading: David Hawke, *In the Midst of a Revolution* (Philadelphia, 1961).

Sect. 6. Every freeman of the full age of twenty-one years, having resided in this state for the space of one whole year next before the day of election for representatives, and paid public taxes during that time, shall enjoy the right of an elector: Provided always, that sons of freeholders of the age of twenty-one years shall be intitled to vote although they have not paid taxes.

Sect. 7. The house of representatives of the freemen of this commonwealth shall consist of persons most noted for wisdom and virtue, to be chosen by the freemen of every city and county of this commonwealth respectively. And no person shall be elected unless he has resided in the city or county for which he shall be chosen two years immediately before the said election; nor shall any member, while he continues such, hold any other office, except in the militia.

Sect. 8. No person shall be capable of being elected a member to serve in the house of representatives of the freemen of this commonwealth more than four years in seven. . . .

Sect. 19. For the present the supreme executive council of this state shall consist of twelve persons. . . .

No member of the general assembly or delegate in congress, shall be chosen a member of the council. The president and vice-president shall be chosen annually by the joint ballot of the general assembly and council, of the members of the council. Any person having served as a counsellor for three successive years, shall be incapable of holding that office for four years afterwards. Every member of the council shall be a justice of the peace for the whole commonwealth, by virture of his office.

In case new additional counties shall hereafter be erected in this state, such county or counties shall elect a counsellor, and such county or counties shall be annexed to the next neighbouring counties, and shall take rotation with such counties.

The council shall meet annually, at the same time and place with the general assembly.

The treasurer of the state, trustees of the loan office, naval officers, collectors of customs or excise, judge of the admiralty, attornies general, sheriffs, and prothonotaries, shall not be capable of a seat in the general assembly, executive council, or continental congress.

Sect. 20. The president, and in his absence the vice-president, with the council, five of whom shall be a quorum, shall have power to appoint and commissionate judges, naval officers, judge of the admiralty, attorney general and all other officers, civil and military, except such as are chosen by the general assembly or the people, agreeable to this frame of government, and the laws that may be made hereafter. . . .

Sect. 47. In order that the freedom of the commonwealth may be preserved inviolate forever, there shall be chosen by ballot by the freemen in each city and county respectively, on the second Tuesday in October, in the year one thousand seven hundred and eighty-three, and on the second Tuesday in October, in every seventh year thereafter, two persons in each city and county of this state, to be called the COUNCIL OF CENSORS; who shall meet together on the second Monday of November next ensuing their election; the majority of whom shall be a quorum in every case, except as to calling a convention, in which two-thirds of the whole number elected shall agree: And whose duty it shall be to enquire whether the constitution has been preserved inviolate in every part; and whether the legislative and executive branches of government have performed their duty as guardians of the people, or assumed to themselves, or exercised other or greater powers than they are intitled to by the constitution: They are also to enquire whether the public taxes have been justly laid and collected in all parts of this commonwealth, in what manner the public monies have been disposed of, and whether the laws have been duly executed. For these purposes they shall have power to send for persons, papers, and records; they shall have authority to pass public censures, to order impeachments, and to recommend to the legislature the repealing such laws as appear to them to have been enacted contrary to the principles of the constitution. These powers they shall continue to have, for and during the space of one year from the day of their election and no longer: The said council of censors shall also have power to call a convention, to meet within two years after their sitting, if there appear to them an absolute necessity of amending any article of the constitution which may be defective, explaining such as may be thought not clearly expressed, and of adding such as are necessary for the preservation of the rights and happiness of the people: But the articles to be amended, and the amendments proposed, and such articles as are proposed to be added or abolished, shall be promulgated at least six months before the day appointed for the election of such convention, for the previous consideration of the people, that they may have an opportunity of instructing their delegates on the subject.

Passed in Convention the 28th day of September, 1776, and signed by their order.

Benj. Franklin, Prest.

4. New York Constitution (1777)*

In contrast with Pennsylvania, New York adopted a state constitution one year later that was noted for its conservatism. The chief innovation of this instrument was the Council of Revision, whereby the governor and the highest judges in the state were given the power to revise "all bills about to be passed into laws by the legislature." This was judicial review with a vengeance! Thus the New York Constitution gave to the high judiciary an active role in the legislative process. Judicial review as developed by the U.S. Supreme Court in Marbury v. Madison *(see Document 8), and in most of the states in the first decades of the nineteenth century, was by contrast much more modest in scope, in that it limited the judicial power to the adjudication of actual "cases and controversies" brought by litigants, both public and private. The latter, more normative, model of judicial review gave the courts a role that was more passive than that exemplified by New York's Council of Revision. What are the strengths and weaknesses of these two alternative models of judicial review? Which is more in keeping with a system of separated powers?*

III. And whereas laws inconsistent with the spirit of this constitution, or with the public good, may be hastily and unadvisedly passed: Be it ordained, that the governor for the time being, the chancellor, and the judges of the supreme court, or any two of them, together with the governor, shall be, and hereby are, constituted a council to revise all bills about to be passed into laws by the legislature; and for that purpose shall assemble themselves from time to time, when the legislature shall be convened; for which, nevertheless, they shall not receive any salary or consideration, under any pretence whatever. And that all bills which have passed the senate and assembly shall, before they become laws, be presented to the said council for their revisal and consideration; and if, upon such revision and consideration, it should appear improper to the said council, or a majority of them, that the said bill should become a law of this State, that they return the same, together with their objections thereto in writing, to the senate or house of assembly (in whichsoever the same shall have originated) who shall enter the objection sent down by the council at large in their minutes, and proceed to reconsider the said bill. But if, after such reconsideration, two-thirds of the said senate or house of assembly shall, notwithstanding the said

---

*Available in Thorpe, *Federal and State Constitutions*, Vol. 5.

For further reading: E. Wilder Spaulding, *New York in the Critical Period, 1783–1789* (New York, 1963; originally published 1932), chap. 5.

objections, agree to pass the same, it shall, together with the objections, be sent to the other branch of the legislature, where it shall also be reconsidered, and, if approved by two-thirds of the members present, shall be a law....

XVII. And this convention doth further, in the name and by the authority of the good people of this State, ordain, determine, and declare that the supreme executive power and authority of this State shall be vested in a governor; and that statedly, once in every three years, and as often as the seat of government shall become vacant, a wise and discreet freeholder of this State shall be, by ballot, elected governor, by the freeholders of this State, qualified, as before described, to elect senators; which elections shall be always held at the times and places of choosing representatives in assembly for each respective county; and that the person who hath the greatest number of votes within the said State shall be governor thereof.

XVIII. That the governor shall continue in office three years, and shall, by virtue of his office, be general and commander-in-chief of all the militia, and admiral of the navy of this State; that he shall have power to convene the assembly and senate on extraordinary occasions; to prorogue them from time to time, provided such prorogations shall not exceed sixty days in the space of any one year; and, at his discretion, to grant reprieves and pardons to persons convicted of crimes, other than treason or murder, in which he may suspend the execution of the sentence, until it shall be reported to the legislature at their subsequent meeting; and they shall either pardon or direct the execution of the criminal, or grant a further reprieve.

XIX. That it shall be the duty of the governor to inform the legislature, at every session, of the condition of the State, so far as may respect his department; to recommend such matters to their consideration as shall appear to him to concern its good government, welfare, and prosperity; to correspond with the Continental Congress, and other States; to transact all necessary business with the officers of government, civil and military; to take care that the laws are faithfully executed to the best of his ability; and to expedite all such measures as may be resolved upon by the legislature....

XXIV. That all military officers be appointed during pleasure; that all commissioned officers, civil and military, be commissioned by the governor; and that the chancellor, the judges of the supreme court, and first judge of the county court in every county, hold their offices during good behavior or until they shall have respectively attained the age of sixty years.

5. Articles of Confederation (1781)*

The Articles of Confederation were much more than a feeble first step on the road to federal union. Drafted, signed, and ratified during the Revolution, the Articles showed how far the new sovereign states were prepared to go in surrendering portions of their sovereignty without giving up the independence for which the American states were fighting. In comparison to the United States Constitution, the Articles created a weak central government. This should not be surprising; the revolutionary generation, in the process of overthrowing British imperial domination, was not inclined to substitute one strong central government for another. What is significant is the amount of power the states willingly surrendered under the Articles, rather than the sovereign authority they retained. Analyze the four articles reproduced below (there were thirteen altogether), and then list the powers granted to the United States Congress under the Articles. Of particular interest is Article IV, which, among other things, proscribed any state from imposing restrictions that would "prevent the removal of property [i.e., black slaves] imported into any state, to any other state of which the Owner is an inhabitant." This restriction on state power shows that the slaveholding interest was not always identified with "states' rights." Explain.

Article I. The Stile of this Confederacy shall be "The United States of America."

Article II. Each state retains its sovereignty, freedom, and independence, and every Power, Jurisdiction and right, which is not by this confederation expressly delegated to the United States, in Congress assembled.

Article III. The said states hereby severally enter into a firm league of friendship with each other, for their common defence, the security of their Liberties, and their mutual and general welfare, binding themselves to assist each other, against all force offered to, or attacks made upon them, or any of them, on account of religion, sovereignty, trade, or any other pretence whatever.

Article IV. The better to secure and perpetuate mutual friendship and intercourse among the people of the different states in this union, the free inhabitants of each of these states, paupers, vagabonds and fugitives from justice excepted, shall be entitled to all privileges and

---

*Articles of Confederation and perpetual Union between the states... Available in Commager, *Documents of American History,* vol. 1.

For further reading: Merrill Jensen, *The Articles of Confederation: An Interpretation of the Social Constitutional History of the American Revolution, 1774–1781* (Madison, Wisc., 1940).

immunities of free citizens in the several states; and the people of each state shall have free ingress and regress to and from any other state, and shall enjoy therein all the privileges of trade and commerce, subject to the same duties, impositions and restrictions as the inhabitants thereof respectively, provided that such restrictions shall not extend so far as to prevent the removal of property imported into any state, to any other state of which the Owner is an inhabitant; provided also that no imposition, duties or restrictions shall be laid by any state, on the property of the united states, or either of them.

If any Person guilty of, or charged with treason, felony, or other high misdemeanor in any state, shall flee from Justice, and be found in any of the united states, he shall, upon demand of the Governor or executive power, of the state from which he fled, be delivered up and removed to the state having jurisdiction of his offence.

Full faith and credit shall be given in each of these states to the records, acts and judicial proceedings of the courts and magistrates of every other state....

6. United States Constitution (1787)*

Because the Constitution, as amended, has been the supreme law of the land since 1789, every word and phrase of that document has been construed in exhaustive detail by historians, lawyers, jurists, and legislators. (A useful one-volume compendium of much of this learning can be found in the 1972 edition of the annotated Constitution: The Constitution of the United States of America: Analysis and Interpretation [*Washington, D.C., 1973*]. The Constitution ought to be viewed not simply as an improvement over the Articles of Confederation but as a completely different instrument with a wholly distinctive conceptual basis. Under the Articles of Confederation, the central government enjoyed only such power as the states surrendered. It was a creature of the states. Enforcement of federal law was very much dependent on state cooperation and compliance. In contrast, the United States government under the Constitution was the creation of the people of the United States. Its laws were enforceable directly through federal courts. Whereas the natural evolution of the Articles of*

---

* The Constitution of the United States of America. Proposed by Convention, September 17, 1787; effective March 14, 1789. Available in Commager, *Documents of American History*, vol. 1.

   For further reading: Gordon S. Wood, *The Creation of the American Republic, 1776-1787* (Chapel Hill, N.C., 1969).

Confederation would have been toward a parliamentary system of government, the Constitution established a presidential system with a powerful chief executive elected independently of the legislative branch. Indeed, the most original creation of the framers of the Constitution was the electoral college apparatus for choosing the President, which, until adoption of the Twelfth Amendment, appeared as it is reproduced below. Can you think of reasons why the framers chose such an awkward and seemingly cumbersome system of election? Why did they not simply require election by Congress or by the people directly? Compare the office of the presidency with the powers of the governor of New York (see Document 4). Are the reasons for having a strong executive at the state level the same as those for having a strong executive at the national level?

ARTICLE II

Section 1. The executive Power shall be vested in a President of the United States of America. He shall hold his Office during the Term of four Years, and, together with the Vice President, chosen for the same Term, be elected, as follows.

Each State shall appoint, in such manner as the Legislature thereof may direct, a Number of Electors, equal to the whole Number of Senators and Representatives to which the State may be entitled in the Congress: but no Senator or Representative, or Person holding an Office of Trust or Profit under the United States, shall be appointed an Elector.

The Electors shall meet in their respective States, and vote by Ballot for two Persons, of whom one at least shall not be an inhabitant of the same State with themselves. And they shall make a List of all the Persons voted for, and of the Number of Votes for each; which List they shall sign and certify, and transmit sealed to the Seat of the Government of the United States, directed to the President of the Senate. The President of the Senate shall, in the Presence of the Senate and House of Representatives, open all the Certificates, and the Votes shall then be counted. The Person having the greatest Number of Votes shall be the President, if such Number be a Majority of the whole Number of Electors appointed; and if there be more than one who have such Majority, and have an equal Number of Votes, then the House of Representatives shall immediately chuse by Ballot one of them for President; and if no Person have a Majority, then from the five highest on the List the said House shall in like Manner chuse the President. But in chusing the President, the Votes shall be taken by States, the Representation from each State having one Vote; A quorum for this

Purpose shall consist of a Member or Members from two thirds of the States, and a Majority of all the States shall be necessary to a Choice. In every Case, after the Choice of the President, the Person having the greatest Number of Votes of the Electors shall be the Vice President. But if there should remain two or more who have equal votes, the Senate shall chuse from them by Ballot the Vice President.

The Congress may determine the Time of chusing the Electors, and the Day on which they shall give their Votes; which Day shall be the same throughout the United States....

Section 2. The President shall be Commander in Chief of the Army and Navy of the United States, and of the Militia of the several States, when called into the actual Service of the United States; he may require the Opinion, in writing, of the principal Officer in each of the executive Departments, upon any Subject relating to the Duties of their respective Offices, and he shall have Power to grant Reprieves and Pardons for Offences against the United States, except in Cases of Impeachment.

He shall have Power, by and with the Advice and Consent of the Senate, to make Treaties, provided two thirds of the Senators present concur; and he shall nominate, and by and with the Advice and Consent of the Senate, shall appoint Ambassadors, other public Ministers and Consuls, Judges of the supreme Court, and all other Officers of the United States, whose Appointments are not herein otherwise provided for, and which shall be established by Law: but the Congress may by Law vest the Appointment of such inferior Officers, as they think proper, in the President alone, in the Courts of Law, or in the Heads of Departments.

The President shall have Power to fill up all Vacancies that may happen during the Recess of the Senate, by granting Commissions which shall expire at the End of their next Session.

Section 3. He shall from time to time give to the Congress Information of the State of the Union, and recommend to their Consideration such Measures as he shall judge necessary and expedient; he may, on extraordinary Occasions, convene both Houses, or either of them, and in Case of Disagreement between them, with Respect to the Time of Adjournment, he may adjourn them to such Time as he shall think proper; he shall receive Ambassadors and other public Ministers; he shall take Care that the Laws be faithfully executed, and shall Commission all the Officers of the United States.

7. Virginia Declaration of Rights (1776)*

The Virginia Declaration of Rights, a model for other states' bills of rights as well as for the federal Bill of Rights (Amendments 1-10 of the Constitution), shows a shifting focus and a rhythmic variation between broad statements of political philosophy (paragraphs 1-7, 15-16) and narrower legal concerns (paragraphs 8-14). Most of the states' bills of rights contained a similar binocular focus. The federal Bill of Rights did not, however. Can you think of reasons why Congress, in drafting the first ten amendments to the Constitution refrained from statements of political philosophy and concentrated instead on a particularized enumeration of legal guarantees of personal rights?

A DECLARATION OF RIGHTS MADE BY THE REPRESENTATIVES OF THE GOOD PEOPLE OF VIRGINIA, ASSEMBLED IN FULL AND FREE CONVENTION; WHICH RIGHTS DO PERTAIN TO THEM AND THEIR POSTERITY, AS THE BASIS AND FOUNDATION OF GOVERNMENT.

Sec. 1. That all men are by nature equally free and independent, and have certain inherent rights, of which, when they enter into a state of society, they cannot by any compact deprive or divest their posterity; namely, the enjoyment of life and liberty, with the means of acquiring and possessing property, and pursuing and obtaining happiness and safety.

Sec. 2. That all power is vested in, and consequently derived from, the people; that magistrates are their trustees and servants, and at all times amenable to them.

Sec. 3. That government is, or ought to be instituted for the common benefit, protection, and security of the people, nation, or community; of all the various modes and forms of government, that is best which is capable of producing the greatest degree of happiness and safety, and is most effectually secured against the danger of maladministration; and that when any government shall be found inadequate or contrary to these purposes, a majority of the community hath an indubitable,

* A Declaration of Rights made by the representatives of the good people of Virginia ... Adopted by the Virginia Convention, 1776. Available in Commager, *Documents of American History,* vol. 1.
  For further reading: Helen Hill, *George Mason, Constitutionalist* (Cambridge, Mass., 1938), chap. 10.

unalienable and indefeasible right to reform, alter or abolish it, in such manner as shall be judged most conducive to the public weal.

Sec. 4. That no man, or set of men, are entitled to exclusive or separate emoluments or privileges from the community, but in consideration of publick services; which, not being descendible, neither ought the offices of magistrate, legislator or judge to be hereditary.

Sec. 5. That the legislative and executive powers of the state should be separate and distinct from the judiciary; and that the members of the two first may be restrained from oppression, by feeling and participating the burthens of the people, they should, at fixed periods, be reduced to a private station, return into that body from which they were originally taken, and the vacancies be supplied by frequent, certain, and regular elections, in which all, or any part of the former members to be again eligible or ineligible, as the laws shall direct.

Sec. 6. That elections of members to serve as representatives of the people in assembly, ought to be free; and that all men having sufficient evidence of permanent common interest with, and attachment to the community, have the right of suffrage, and cannot be taxed or deprived of their property for publick uses, without their own consent, or that of their representatives so elected, nor bound by any law to which they have not, in like manner, assented for the public good.

Sec. 7. That all power of suspending laws, or the execution of laws, by an authority without consent of the representatives of the people, is injurious to their rights, and ought not to be exercised.

Sec. 8. That in all capital or criminal prosecutions a man hath a right to demand the cause and nature of his accusation, to be confronted with the accusers and witnesses, to call for evidence in his favour, and to a speedy trial by an impartial jury of his vicinage, without whose unanimous consent he cannot be found guilty; nor can he be compelled to give evidence against himself; that no man be deprived of his liberty, except by the law of the land or the judgment of his peers.

Sec. 9. That excessive bail ought not to be required, nor excessive fines imposed, nor cruel and unusual punishments inflicted.

Sec. 10. That general warrants, whereby an officer or messenger may be commanded to search suspected places without evidence of a fact committed, or to seize any person or persons not named, or whose offence is not particularly described and supported by evidence, are grievous and oppressive, and ought not to be granted.

Sec. 11. That in controversies respecting property, and in suits between man and man, the ancient trial by jury is preferable to any other, and ought to be held sacred.

Sec. 12. That the freedom of the press is one of the great bulwarks of liberty, and can never be restrained but by despotick governments.

Sec. 13. That a well-regulated militia, composed of the body of the people trained to arms, is the proper, natural and safe defence of a free state; that standing armies in time of peace should be avoided as dangerous to liberty; and that in all cases the military should be under strict subordination to, and governed by, the civil power.

Sec. 14. That the people have a right to uniform government; and, therefore, that no government separate from, or independent of the government of Virginia, ought to be erected or established within the limits thereof.

Sec. 15. That no free government, or the blessings of liberty, can be preserved to any people, but by a firm adherence to justice, moderation, temperance, frugality and virtue, and by frequent recurrence to fundamental principles.

Sec. 16. That religion, or the duty which we owe to our Creator, and the manner of discharging it, can be directed only by reason and conviction, not by force or violence; and therefore all men are equally entitled to the free exercise of religion, according to the dictates of conscience; and that it is the mutual duty of all to practise Christian forbearance, love, and charity towards each other.

8. Marbury v. Madison (1803)*

The logic of Chief Justice John Marshall in Marbury v. Madison *now appears to be inescapable. When ordinary legislative acts are in conflict with the supreme law of the land, the ordinary act must give way to the constitutional mandate. Most of Marshall's contemporaries would not have objected to that simple proposition. But who was to decide when and if there was such a conflict? Marshall concluded that this was the preeminent responsibility of the Supreme Court, but his critics did not agree. If that was the Court's responsibility, they asked, then why did the framers of the Constitution not so provide in Article III, when they established the jurisdiction of the federal judicial power? In reaching his conclusion, Marshall advanced a series of hypotheticals—examples of laws such as tariffs on exports and ex post facto laws that courts should not enforce because they are contrary to the explicit language of the Constitution. These examples are so simple that they are self-evident. Can you think of other*

* 5 U.S. (1 Cranch) 137 (1803). Available in Commager, *Documents of American History,* vol. 1.

For further reading: Robert G. McCloskey, *The American Supreme Court* (Chicago, 1960).

hypothetical examples where judges might very well and justifiably "close their eyes on the constitution, and see only the law"? Marshall conceded that Congress, and indeed all of the departments of the government, are bound by the Constitution. Why, then, should the Court's interpretation of that instrument prevail in a government of coequal but separate branches?

MARSHALL, C.J.

The question, whether an act, repugnant to the constitution, can become the law of the land, is a question deeply interesting to the United States; but, happily, not of an intricacy proportioned to its interest. It seems only necessary to recognize certain principles, supposed to have been long and well established, to decide it.

That the people have an original right to establish, for their future government, such principles as, in their opinion, shall most conduce to their own happiness, is the basis on which the whole American fabric has been erected. The exercise of this original right is a very great exertion; nor can it, nor ought it, to be frequently repeated. The principles, therefore, so established, are deemed fundamental. And as the authority from which they proceed is supreme, and can seldom act, they are designed to be permanent.

This original and supreme will organizes the government, and assigns to different departments their respective powers. It may either stop here, or establish certain limits not to be transcended by those departments.

The government of the United States is of the latter description. The powers of the legislature are defined and limited; and that those limits may not be mistaken, or forgotten, the constitution is written. To what purpose are powers limited, and to what purpose is that limitation committed to writing, if these limits may, at any time, be passed by those intended to be restrained? The distinction between a government with limited and unlimited powers is abolished, if those limits do not confine the persons on whom they are imposed, and if acts prohibited and acts allowed, are of equal obligation. It is a proposition too plain to be contested, that the constitution controls any legislative act repugnant to it; or, that the legislature may alter the constitution by an ordinary act.

Between these alternatives there is no middle ground. The constitution is either a superior, paramount law, unchangeable by ordinary means, or it is on a level with ordinary legislative acts, and, like other acts, is alterable when the legislature shall please to alter it.

If the former part of the alternative be true, then a legislative act contrary to the constitution is not law: if the latter part be true, then written constitutions are absurd attempts, on the part of the people, to limit a power in its own nature illimitable.

Certainly all those who have framed written constitutions contemplate them as forming the fundamental and paramount law of the nation, and consequently, the theory of every such government must be, that an act of the legislature, repugnant to the constitution, is void.

This theory is essentially attached to a written constitution, and is, consequently, to be considered, by this court, as one of the fundamental principles of our society. It is not therefore to be lost sight of in the further consideration of this subject.

If an act of the legislature, repugnant to the constitution, is void, does it, notwithstanding its invalidity, bind the courts, and oblige them to give it effect? Or, in other words, though it be not law, does it constitute a rule as operative as if it was a law? This would be to overthrow in fact what was established in theory; and would seem, at first view, an absurdity too gross to be insisted on. It shall, however, receive a more attentive consideration.

It is emphatically the province and duty of the judicial department to say what the law is. Those who apply the rule to particular cases, must of necessity expound and interpret that rule. If two laws conflict with each other, the courts must decide on the operation of each.

So if a law be in opposition to the constitution; if both the law and the constitution apply to a particular case, so that the court must either decide that case conformably to the law, disregarding the constitution; or conformably to the constitution, disregarding the law; the court must determine which of these conflicting rules governs the case. This is of the very essence of judicial duty.

If then the courts are to regard the constitution; and the constitution is superior to any ordinary act of the legislature; the constitution, and not such ordinary act, must govern the case to which they both apply.

Those then who controvert the principle that the constitution is to be considered, in court, as a paramount law, are reduced to the necessity of maintaining that courts must close their eyes on the constitution, and see only the law.

This doctrine would subvert the very foundation of all written constitutions. It would declare that an act, which, according to the principles and theory of our government, is entirely void; is yet, in practice, completely obligatory. It would declare, that if the legislature shall do what is expressly forbidden, such act, notwithstanding the express prohibition, is in reality effectual. It would be giving to the legislature a practical and real omnipotence, with the same breath which professes to restrict their powers within narrow limits, and declaring that those limits may be passed at pleasure.

That it thus reduces to nothing what we have deemed the greatest improvement on political institutions—a written constitution—would of itself be sufficient, in America, where written constitutions have been viewed with so much reverence, for rejecting the construction....

It is declared that "no tax or duty shall be laid on articles exported from any state." Suppose a duty on the export of cotton, of tobacco, or of flour; and a suit instituted to recover it. Ought judgment to be rendered in such a case? Ought the judges to close their eyes on the constitution, and only see the law?

The constitution declares that "no bill of attainder or *ex post facto* law shall be passed."

If, however, such a bill should be passed, and a person should be prosecuted under it; must the court condemn to death those victims whom the constitution endeavors to preserve?....

From these, and many other selections which might be made, it is apparent, that the framers of the constitution contemplated that instrument, as a rule for the government of *courts,* as well as of the legislature....

It is also not entirely unworthy of observation, that in declaring what shall be the *supreme* law of the land, the *constitution* itself is first mentioned; and not the laws of the United States generally, but those only which shall be made in *pursuance* of the constitution, have that rank.

Thus, the particular phraseology of the constitution of the United States confirms and strengthens the principle, supposed to be essential to all written constitutions, that a law repugnant to the constitution is void; and that *courts,* as well as other departments, are bound by that instrument.

9. Madison's Memorial and Remonstrance (1785)*

The Memorial and Remonstrance *is one of the "great documents" of religious freedom in American history. James Madison drafted it in opposition to a proposed statute that would have levied a property tax for the purpose of supporting Christian ministers and teachers. Madison's critics accused him and his supporters of atheism because of their opposition to the measure; but as the* Remonstrance *makes clear, Madison had as much right to claim that he was defending true belief as did his critics. The* Remonstrance *is particularly interesting because it contains within it elements of Madison's political philosophy. Indeed, both Jefferson and Madison derived some of their basic political principles from their fight for separation of church and state in Virginia. What elements of political philosophy are woven into the fabric of this argument for church-state separation? Here Madison was opposing the allocation of tax revenues for the support of religious institutions. Do you think he would have been equally offended by a policy that simply exempted all church property from taxation?*

To the Honorable the General Assembly of the Commonwealth of Virginia

We the subscribers, citizens of the said Commonwealth, having taken into serious consideration, a Bill, printed by order of the last Session of General Assembly, entitled "A Bill establishing a provision for Teachers of the Christian Religion," and conceiving that the same, if finally armed with the sanctions of a law, will be a dangerous abuse of power, are bound, as faithful members of a free State, to remonstrate against it, and to declare the reasons by which we are determined. We remonstrate against the said Bill:

1. Because we hold it for fundamental and undeniable truth, "that Religion, or the duty which we owe to the Creator, and the manner of discharging it, can be directed only by reason and conviction, not by force or violence." The Religion, then, of every man must be left to the conviction and conscience of every man; and it is the right of every man to exercise it as these may dictate. This right is, in its nature, an unalienable right. It is unalienable, because the opinions of men

---

* Memorial and Remonstrance Against Religious Assessments. Available in *The Papers of James Madison,* W.T. Hutchinson et al. (eds.), 13 vols. to date (Chicago, 1962–), vol. 8.

For further reading: Thomas E. Buckley, S.J., *Church and State in Revolutionary Virginia, 1776–1787* (Charlottesville, Va., 1977).

depending only on the evidence contemplated by their own minds, cannot follow the dictates of other men. It is unalienable, also, because what is here a right towards man is a duty towards the Creator. It is the duty of every man to render to the Creator such homage, and such only, as he believes to be acceptable to him. This duty is precedent, both in order of time and in degree of obligation, to the claims of Civil Society. Before any man can be considered as a member of Civil Society he must be considered as a subject of the Governor of the Universe. And if a member of Civil Society who enters into any subordinate Association must always do it with a reservation of his duty to the General Authority, much more must every man who becomes a member of any particular Civil Society do it with a saving of his allegiance to the Universal Sovereign. We maintain, therefore, that in matters of Religion, no man's right is abridged by the institution of Civil Society, and that Religion is wholly exempt from its cognizance. True it is that no other rule exists by which any question which may divide a Society can be ultimately determined but by the will of the majority. But it is also true that the majority may trespass on the rights of the minority.

2. Because, if Religion be exempt from the authority of the Society at large, still less can it be subject to that of the Legislative Body. The latter are but the creatures and viceregents of the former. Their jurisdiction is both derivative and limited. It is limited with regard to the coordinate departments; more necessarily is it limited with regard to the con-stituents. The preservation of a free Government requires not merely that the metes and bounds which separate each department of power be invariably maintained, but more especially that neither of them be suffered to overleap the great Barrier which defends the rights of the people. The Rulers who are guilty of such encroachment exceed the commission from which they derive their authority, and are Tyrants. The people who submit to it are governed by laws made neither by themselves nor by an authority derived from them, and are slaves.

3. Because it is proper to take alarm at the first experiment on our liberties. We behold this prudent jealousy to be the first duty of Citizens and one of the noblest characteristics of the late Revolution. The freemen of America did not wait till usurped power had strengthened itself by exercise and entangled the question in precedents. They saw all the consequences in the principle, and they avoided the consequences by denying the principle. We revere this lesson too much soon to forget it. Who does not see that the same authority which can establish Christianity, in exclusion of all other Religions, may establish with the

same ease any particular sect of Christians in exclusion of all other Sects? That the same authority which can force a citizen to contribute three pence only of his property for the support of any one establishment may force him to conform to any other establishment in all cases whatsoever?

4. Because, the Bill violates that equality which ought to be the basis of every law. . . . If "all men are by nature equally free and independent," all men are to be considered as entering into Society on equal conditions; as relinquishing no more, and therefore retaining no less, one than another, of their natural rights. Above all are they to be considered as retaining an "*equal* title to the free exercise of Religion according to the dictates of Conscience." Whilst we assert for ourselves a freedom to embrace, to profess and to observe the Religion which we believe to be of divine origin, we cannot deny an equal freedom to those whose minds have not yet yielded to the evidence which has convinced us. If this freedom be abused, it is an offence against God, not against man: To God, therefore, not to men, must an account of it be rendered. As the Bill violates equality by subjecting some to peculiar burdens, so it violates the same principle, by granting to others peculiar exemptions. Are the Quakers and Menonists the only sects who think a compulsive support of their Religions unnecessary and unwarrantable? Can their piety alone be intrusted with the care of public worship? Ought their Religions to be endowed above all others, with extraordinary privileges, by which proselytes may be enticed from all others? We think too favorably of the justice and good sense of these denominations, to believe that they either covet preeminencies over their fellow citizens, or that they will be seduced by them, from the common opposition to the measure. . . .

6. Because the establishment proposed by the Bill is not requisite for the support of the Christian Religion. To say that it is, is a contradiction to the Christian Religion itself; for every page of it disavows a dependence on the powers of this world: it is a contradiction to fact; for it is known that this Religion both existed and flourished, not only without the support of human laws, but in spite of every opposition from them; and not only during the period of miraculous aid, but long after it had been left to its own evidence, and the ordinary care of Providence: Nay, it is a contradiction in terms; for a Religion not invented by human policy, must have preexisted and been supported, before it was established by human policy. It is moreover to weaken in those who profess this Religion a pious confidence in its innate

excellence, and the patronage of its Author; and to foster in those who still reject it, a suspicion that its friends are too conscious of its fallacies, to trust it to its own merits. . . .

10. Virginia Religious Freedom Act (1786)*

In the Religious Freedom Bill which he authored, Thomas Jefferson wrote: "truth is great and will prevail if left to herself . . . she is the proper and sufficient antagonist to error . . . [which ceases] to be dangerous when [truth] is permitted freely to contradict [it]." Fifteen years later, in his first inaugural address, Jefferson said: "[E]rror of opinion may be tolerated where reason is left free to combat it." While the words are almost the same, Jefferson in his presidential address was speaking about secular liberties, particularly freedom of speech and of the press; in the statute of 1786 his concern was religious liberty and freedom of conscience. What are the links connecting religious freedom and secular liberty? What reasons did Jefferson offer in the Virginia statute itself for religious disestablishment? Identify the constitutional problem the statute addresses in section 3.

I. Whereas, Almighty God hath created the mind free; that all attempts to influence it by temporal punishments or burthens, or by civil incapacitations, tend only to beget habits of hypocrisy and meanness, and are a departure from the plan of the Holy author of our religion, who being Lord both of body and mind, yet chose not to propagate it by coercions on either, as was in his Almighty power to do; that the impious presumption of legislators and rulers, civil as well as ecclesiastical, who being themselves but fallible and uninspired men, have assumed dominion over the faith of others, setting up their own opinions and modes of thinking as the only true and infallible, and as such endeavouring to impose them on others, hath established and maintained false religions over the greatest part of the world, and through all time; that to compel a man to furnish contributions of money for the propagation of opinions which he disbelieves, is sinful and tyrannical; that even the forcing him to support this or that teacher of his own

---

* An Act for Establishing Religious Freedom. Adopted January 16, 1786. W.W. Hening (ed.), *Statutes at Large of Virginia* (1823), vol. 12, p. 84. Available in Commager, *Documents of American History*, vol. 1.

For further reading: Dumas Malone, *Jefferson the Virginian* (Boston, 1948), chap. 20.

religious persuasion, is depriving him of the comfortable liberty of giving his contributions to the particular pastor whose morals he would make his pattern, and whose powers he feels most persuasive to righteousness, and is withdrawing from the ministry those temporary rewards, which proceeding from an approbation of their personal conduct, are an additional incitement to earnest and unremitting labours for the instruction of mankind; that our civil rights have no dependence on our religious opinions, any more than our opinions in physics or geometry; that therefore the proscribing any citizen as unworthy the public confidence by laying upon him an incapacity of being called to offices of trust and emolument, unless he profess or renounce this or that religious opinion, is depriving him injuriously of those privileges and advantages to which in common with his fellow-citizens he has a natural right; that it tends only to corrupt the principles of that religion it is meant to encourage, by bribing with a monopoly of worldly honours and emoluments, those who will externally profess and conform to it; that though indeed these are criminal who do not withstand such temptation, yet neither are those innocent who lay the bait in their way; that to suffer the civil magistrate to intrude his powers into the field of opinion, and to restrain the profession or propagation of principles on supposition of their ill tendency, is a dangerous fallacy, which at once destroys all religious liberty, because he being of course judge of that tendency will make his opinions the rule of judgment, and approve or condemn the sentiments of others only as they shall square with or differ from his own; that it is time enough for the rightful purposes of civil government, for its officers to interfere when principles break out into overt acts against peace and good order; and finally, that truth is great and will prevail if left to herself, that she is the proper and sufficient antagonist to error, and has nothing to fear from the conflict, unless by human interposition disarmed of her natural weapons, free argument and debate, errors ceasing to be dangerous when it is permitted freely to contradict them.

II. *Be it enacted by the General Assembly,* that no man shall be compelled to frequent or support any religious worship, place, or ministry whatsoever, nor shall be enforced, restrained, molested, or burthened in his body or goods, nor shall otherwise suffer on account of his religious opinions or belief; but that all men shall be free to profess, and by argument to maintain, their opinion in matters of religion, and that the same shall in no wise diminish, enlarge, or affect their civil capacities.

III. And though we well know that this assembly, elected by the people for the ordinary purposes of legislation only, have no power to restrain the acts of succeeding assemblies, constituted with powers equal to our own, and that therefore to declare this act to be irrevocable would be of no effect in law; yet we are free to declare, and do declare, that the rights hereby asserted are of the natural rights of mankind, and that if any act shall be hereafter passed to repeal the present, or to narrow its operation, such act will be an infringement of natural right.

11. Land Ordinance (1785)*

The Land Ordinance of 1785 established the system by which public lands owned by the federal government were sold to private parties. It was, in short, the cornerstone of the policy of privatization as it affected the public domain. The act had four main elements: (1) rectangular survey (2) sale at auction with public bidding (3) minimum base price per acre, and (4) reservation of designated lots for public schools. The ordinance was enacted at a time when the Confederation was desperate for revenue. Since the ordinance imposed no requirement that purchasers occupy the land and put no upper limit on the amount of acreage which could be purchased at the auction sale, it encouraged speculation in land and the commercialization of the public domain. While the ordinance did set a minimum price of one dollar an acre, the fact that public land could be bought with depreciated paper currency meant that it established a cheap land policy at least until a sound monetary system developed under Treasury Secretary Alexander Hamilton in the 1790s. Still, the ordinance was a clear defeat for prosettler or "squatter" groups. Not until after 1830 did Congress enact preemption laws in response to such demands. How did the ordinance of 1785 reflect the growing force of privatization? What other motivations might there have been for its adoption?

Be it ordained by the United States in Congress assembled, that the territory ceded by individual States to the United States, which has been purchased of the Indian inhabitants, shall be disposed of in the following manner:

---

* An Ordinance for ascertaining the mode of disposing of Lands in the Western Territory. Passed May 20, 1785. Source: John C. Fitzpatrick (ed.), *Journals of the Continental Congress, 1774–1789,* (Washington, D.C. 1904–1937), vol. 28, pp. 375ff. Available in Commager, *Documents of American History,* vol. 1.

For further reading: Paul W. Gates, *History of Public Land Law Development* (Washington, D.C., 1968), chap. 4.

A surveyor from each state shall be appointed by Congress, or a Committee of the States, who shall take an oath for the faithful discharge of his duty, before the Geographer of the United States....

The Surveyors, as they are respectively qualified, shall proceed to divide the said territory into townships of six miles square, by lines running due north and south, and others crossing these at right angles, as near as may be, unless where the boundaries of the late Indian purchases may render the same impracticable....

The lines shall be measured with a chain; shall be plainly marked by chaps on the trees, and exactly described on a plat; whereon shall be noted by the surveyor, at their proper distances, all mines, salt-springs, salt-licks and mill-seats, that shall come to his knowledge, and all water courses, mountains and other remarkable and permanent things, over and near which such lines shall pass, and also the quality of the lands.

The plats of the townships respectively, shall be marked by subdivisions into lots of one mile square, or 640 acres, in the same direction as the external lines, and numbered from 1 to 36; always beginning the succeeding range of the lots with the number next to that with which the preceding one concluded....

[T]he commissioners of the loan-office of the several states, who, after giving notice... shall proceed to sell the townships, or fractional parts of townships, at public vendue, in the following manner, viz: The township, or fractional part of a township, N[o.] 1 in the first range, shall be sold entire; and N[o.] 2, in the same range, by lots; and thus in alternate order through the whole of the first range... provided, that none of the lands, within the said territory, be sold under the price of one dollar the acre, to be paid in specie, or loan-office certificates, reduced to specie value, by the scale of depreciation, or certificates of liquidated debts of the United States, including interest, besides the expense of the survey and other charges thereon, which are hereby rated at thirty six dollars the township... on failure of which payment, the said lands shall again be offered for sale....

There shall be reserved the lot N[o.] 16, of every township, for the maintenance of public schools, within the said township; also one third part of all gold, silver, lead and copper mines, to be sold, or otherwise disposed of as Congress shall hereafter direct....

And Whereas Congress... stipulated grants of land to certain officers and soldiers of the late continental army... for complying... with such engagements, Be it ordained, That the secretary of war... determine who are the objects of the above resolutions and engagements . . . and cause the townships, or fractional parts of townships, hereinbefore reserved for the use of the late continental army, to be drawn for in such manner as he shall deem expedient. . . .

12. The Federal Sedition Act (1798)*

The Sedition Act was one of the most draconian measures ever enacted by Congress. Passed by a Congress dominated by the Federalist party, it was aimed at the suppression of a rising chorus of criticism against Federalist policies mounted by the Jeffersonian opposition press. The political motivation behind the Sedition Act is evidenced by the obvious omission, in section 2, of any mention of the Vice President as one of the officials shielded from criticism. Thus by its terms and its necessary implications, the Sedition Act proscribed criticism of the President but not the Vice President. In addition, anticipating a possible defeat of the Federalists at the polls, the act had an expiration date of March 3, 1801, one day before the end of the term of the Federalist President, John Adams. Should the Federalist party become the party of opposition, as indeed it did after 1801, the Sedition Act would no longer be available to be used against them. A major reason for the defeat of the Federalists in the elections of 1800 was their identification with this oppressive statute.

The opponents of the Sedition Act made two constitutional arguments against it. First, the act on its face was contrary to the First Amendment's clear proscriptions on limiting freedom of the press. Second, since Congress had only enumerated powers—that is, powers specifically delegated to it—then, Jeffersonians queried, what was the basis for the enactment of a law that gave federal courts jurisdiction over common-law seditious libel? The act assumed that Congress had the power to enact statutes, such as the Sedition Act, that codified common-law crimes. But, the Jeffersonians reasoned, the Constitution gave no such jurisdiction or power to Congress under Article I. A decade after the expiration of the Sedition Act, the Supreme Court ruled that federal courts could not exercise common-law criminal jurisdiction (U.S. v. Hudson and Goodwin, 11 U.S. [7 Cranch] 32 [1812]).

What defense and other procedural protections were available to a seditious libel defendant under the terms of the Sedition Act? How do the provisions of the act compare with the principles of law for which the Zenger case stood as precedent?

* 5th Cong. 2d sess. Chap. 74, July 14, 1798. Source: U.S. Congress, *Statutes at Large,* Richard Peters (ed.), (Boston, 1848), vol. 1, p. 596. Available in Commager, *Documents of American History,* vol. 1.

For further reading: James M. Smith, *Freedom's Fetters: The Alien and Sedition Laws and American Civil Liberties* (Ithaca, N.Y., 1956).

Sec. 2. *And be it further enacted,* That if any person shall write, print, utter or publish, or shall cause or procure to be written, printed, uttered or published, or shall knowingly and willingly assist or aid in writing, printing, uttering or publishing any false, scandalous and malicious writing or writings against the government of the United States, or either house of the Congress of the United States, or President of the United States, with intent to defame the said government, or either house of the said Congress, or the said President, or to bring them, or either of them, into contempt or disrepute; or to excite against them, or either or any of them, the hatred of the good people of the United States, or to stir up sedition within the United States, or to excite any unlawful combinations therein, for opposing or resisting any law of the United States, ... or to resist, oppose, or defeat any such law or act, or to aid, encourage or abet any hostile designs of any foreign nation against the United States, their people or government, then such person, being thereof convicted before any court of the United States having jurisdiction thereof, shall be punished by a fine not exceeding two thousand dollars, and by imprisonment not exceeding two years.

Sec. 3. *And be it further enacted and declared,* That if any person shall be prosecuted under this act, for the writing or publishing any libel aforesaid, it shall be lawful for the defendant, upon the trial of the cause, to give evidence in his defence, the truth of the matter contained in the publication charged as a libel. And the jury who shall try the cause, shall have a right to determine the law and the fact, under the direction of the court, as in other cases.

Sec. 4. *And be it further enacted,* That this act shall continue and be in force until the third day of March, one thousand eight hundred and one, and no longer: *Provided,* that the expiration of the act shall not prevent or defeat a prosecution and punishment of any offence against the law, during the time it shall be in force.

13. Commonwealth v. Clap (1808)*

Commonwealth v. Clap *is an interesting case that shows the durability of pre-Zenger doctrines of seditious libel. The case recalls the strictures of Sir William Blackstone, who had written that the truth of a libel made it more indefensible*

---

* *Commonwealth v. Clap,* 4 Mass. 163 (1808).

   For further reading: Norman L. Rosenberg, "The Law of Political Libel and Freedom of Press in Nineteenth-Century America: An Interpretation," *American Journal of Legal History,* 17 (1973), 336–352.

than a false libel. In Commonwealth v. Clap, *Chief Justice Parsons allowed truth of the libelous words as evidence to disprove malice and intent, but as a matter of substantive law, he did not allow the truth to be used as an absolute defense to the charge—as it had been in the Zenger case and in cases tried under the Sedition Act. Despite its doctrinal conservatism, however, the case does show the tenor of the times. Parsons placed candidates for elective office outside the normal canons of seditious libel law. By implication, nonelective officials would have the full protection of the law. Why did Parsons make this implicit distinction between elective and nonelective officials? What argument could you make against distinguishing in this way between elected and appointed officials?*

PARSONS, C.J.

The defendant has been convicted, by the verdict of a jury, of publishing a libel. On the trial, he moved to give in evidence, in his defence, that the contents of the publication were true. This evidence the judge rejected, and for that reason, the defendant moves for a new trial.

It is necessary to consider what publication is libellous, and the reason why a libellous publication is an offence against the commonwealth.

A libel is a malicious publication, expressed either in printing or writing, or by signs and pictures, tending either to blacken the memory of one dead, or the reputation of one who is alive, and expose him to public hatred, contempt, or ridicule.

The cause why libellous publications are offences against the state, is their direct tendency to a breach of the public peace, by provoking the parties injured, and their friends and families, to acts of revenge, which it would not be easy to restrain, were offences of this kind not severely punished. And every day's experience will justify the law in attributing to libels that tendency which renders the publication of them an offence against the state. The essence of the offence consists in the malice of the publication, or the intent to defame the reputation of another. In the definition of a libel, as an offence against law, it is not considered whether the publication be true or false; because a man may maliciously publish the truth against another, with the intent to defame his character, and if the publication be true, the tendency of it to inflame the passions, and to excite revenge, is not diminished, but may sometimes be strengthened.

The inference is, therefore, very clear, that the defendant cannot justify himself for publishing a libel, merely by proving the truth of the publication, and that the direction of the judge was right.

If the law admitted the truth of the words in this case to be a justification, the effect would be a greater injury to the party libelled. He is not a party to prosecution, nor is he put on his defence; and the evidence at the trial might more cruelly defame his character than the original libel.

Although the truth of the words is no justification in a criminal prosecution for a libel, yet the defendant may repel the charge, by proving that the publication was for a justifiable purpose, and not malicious, nor with the intent to defame any man. And there may be cases, where the defendant, having proved the purpose justifiable, may give in evidence the truth of the words, when such evidence will tend to negative the malice and intent to defame.

Upon this principle, a man may apply by complaint to the legislature to remove an unworthy officer; and if the complaint be true, and made with the honest intention of giving useful information, and not maliciously, or with intent to defame, the complaint will not be a libel.

And when any man shall consent to be a candidate for a public office conferred by the election of the people, he must be considered as putting his character in issue, so far as it may respect his fitness and qualifications for the office. And publications of the truth on this subject, with the honest intention of informing the people, are not a libel. For it would be unreasonable to conclude that the publication of truths, which it is the interest of the people to know, should be an offence against their laws.

And every man holding a public elective office may be considered as within this principle; for as a reelection is the only way his constituents can manifest their approbation of his conduct, it is to be presumed that he is consenting to a reelection, if he does not disclaim it. For every good man would wish the approbation of his constituents for meritorious conduct.

For the same reason, the publication of falsehood and calumny against public officers, or candidates for public offices, is an offence most dangerous to the people, and deserves punishment, because the people may be deceived, and reject the best citizens, to their great injury, and it may be to the loss of their liberties.

But the publication of a libel maliciously and with intent to defame, whether it be true or not, is clearly an offence against the law, on sound principles, which must be adhered to, so long as the restraint of all tendencies to the breach of the public peace, and to private animosity and revenge, is salutary to the commonwealth.

The defendant took nothing by his motion, and was afterwards sentenced to two months' imprisonment, with costs.

14. *Massachusetts Milldam Act* (1795)*

The Massachusetts Milldam Act of 1795 is one of many similar measures passed in the states in the late eighteenth and early nineteenth centuries to encourage economic development. That encouragement took the form of permitting a mill owner to flood adjacent lands without the permission of adjacent landowners, at the cost of paying an annual damage award. In effect, the act compelled adjacent owners to accept a private "taking" without their consent and without receiving just compensation in the form of a lump sum payment. Outline the procedural requirements of the act. Was the fact that the assessment was to be made by a jury an adequate procedural safeguard for the owners of flooded lands? Can you think of any other procedures that might have been used to accommodate all parties to these lawsuits?

Whereas the erection and support of Mills to accommodate the Inhabitants of the several parts of the State ought not to be discouraged by many doubts and disputes; and some special Provisions are found necessary relative to flowing adjacent lands and mills held by several proprietors — Therefore —

Sec. 1st. *Be it enacted by the Senate and House of Representatives in General Court assembled and by the Authority of the same,* that where any person hath already erected, or shall erect any water Mill on his own land, or on the land of any other person by his consent legally obtained, and to the working of such mill, it shall be found necessary to raise a suitable head of water, and in so doing any lands shall be flowed not belonging to the owner of such mill, it shall be lawfull for the owner or occupant of such mill to continue the same head of water to his best advantage in the manner and on the terms herein after mentioned.

Sec. 2d. *And be it further enacted,* that if any person shall sustain damages in his lands by their being flowed as aforesaid, he may complain to the Court of common pleas of the County wherein the lands so flowed shall be situated and the said Court shall issue a warrant to the

---

* An Act For The Support and Regulation of Mills. Source: Act of February 27, 1796, chap. 74 [1794–96] Mass. Acts and Resolves [1794–1796], chap. 74, p. 443.

For further reading: Morton J. Horwitz, *The Transformation of American Law, 1780–1860* (Cambridge, Mass., 1977).

Sherrif of the same County; and if the Sherrif shall be interested, then to some Coroner of the same County not interested, such Sherrif, or Coroner to be named by the Court, directing him to summon and impanel a jury of twelve good and lawfull men; which jury shall be sworn to make a true and faithfull appraisement of the yearly damages done to the complainant by so flowing his lands, and how far the same may be necessary. And said jury shall try the cause, and their verdict being returned by the officer to the same Court and there allowed and recorded shall be a sufficient bar to any action to be brought for any such damages — And it shall be in the power of said Court to assess such sum to the officer for his services as they may judge reasonable.

Sec. 3d. *And be it further enacted,* that such verdict and judgment thereon so recorded shall be the measure of the yearly damages, untill the owner or occupant of such mill or the owner or occupant of such lands so flowed shall, on a new complaint to the said Court of the County, and by the form of process before prescribed obtain an increase or decrease of the said damages — And the party intitled to any such yearly damages, whether the party to the record his heirs, executors, administrators or assigns may have an action of debt grounded on such record to recover the same — And the party prevailing in any complaint or action aforesaid shall be allowed his full legal costs, though the damages so assessed or debt recovered, shall not amount to the sum of four pounds.

Sec. 4th. *And be it further enacted* that ... when the said jury shall so inquire of the said yearly damages they shall also inquire and make return in their said verdict what portion of the year, the said lands ought not to be so flowed and during such portion of the year as the said jury shall certify in their verdict that the public convenience and the circumstances of the case do not justify such flowing and the said verdict being accepted by the court this act shall, in no manner, authorize the said owner or occupant of such mill so to flow the said lands of others....

15. Stowell v. Flagg (1814)*

In Stowell v. Flagg, *the Massachusetts Supreme Judicial Court made the procedures established under the milldam act the exclusive remedy for adjacent property owners. The court validated the purpose of the act, which was to spare*

* *Stowell v. Flagg,* 11 Mass. 364 (1814).

For further reading: Oscar Handlin and Mary F. Handlin, *Commonwealth: A Study of the Role of Government in the American Economy: Massachusetts, 1774–1861,* rev. ed. (Cambridge, Mass., 1969; originally published 1947), chap. 3.

mill owners the burden of repeated litigation. In so holding, the court also validated the underlying economic and political values the milldam act represented—promotion of the private aggrandizement of some propertied interests at the expense of others. The justification for this partiality was that "the use of the property [by the mill owner]... is supposed to be of public importance." This plus the acknowledgment that the statute was "incautiously copied" suggests that Chief Justice Parker may have had reservations about the milldam act. But these he apparently resolved by deferring to the legislature's wisdom: "As the law is, so we must declare it." What argument could you make that the preservation of the traditional property rights and legal remedies of adjacent owners was as much a matter of "public importance" as relieving mill owners of the burdens of "continual lawsuits and expenses"? Assume that the legislature had rejected the milldam act when it was first proposed. Would this have seriously impeded the development of the early textile industry, since factories employed water power almost exclusively as their principal energy source?

PARKER, C.J.

This is an action of the case at common law, to recover damages by reason of the flowing of the plaintiff's land, occasioned by the erection and continuance of a dam across a stream of water, running through the soil of the defendant; which dam was erected for the purpose of raising a head of water sufficient to carry mills owned and occupied by the defendant.

There is no doubt that such an action lies at common law for this consequential injury, upon the common maxim that every man is so to use his own property as not to injure his neighbor; and if an injury does ensue from an otherwise legitimate use of his own property, he is to compensate his neighbor in damages....

The act of the legislature, entitled "An Act for the support and regulation of mills," seems to have been made with a view to favor the owners of mills, so far as to relieve them from the frequent suits with which they were threatened by the owners of the adjoining soil. The preamble of the act shows this to have been the design of the legislature; and the words of the first section of it go far to establish a right in the owners of mills to flow the adjoining lands, if necessary to the working of their mills; subject only to such damages as shall be ascertained by the particular process therein directed.

As the common law action is founded on a wrong done by the defendant, and the process itself presupposes a tort, when the legislature has authorized the act itself complained of, we cannot conceive that the action remains.

If it should be said that the legislature itself has not the constitutional authority to deprive a citizen of a remedy for a wrong actually done to him, the answer is obvious, that they have a right to substitute one process for another; as, for instance, they may declare that, for an assault and battery, an action of the case shall be brought, instead of an action of trespass; or that the process shall be by complaint, and not by writ.

From the general purview of the statute, made expressly to relieve mill owners from the difficulties and disputes they were before subject to, there can be no doubt of the intention of the legislature to take away the common law action, which might be renewed for every new injury, and so burden the owner of a mill with continual lawsuits and expenses. But as the statute in question is not drawn with technical precision, and as there are several clauses and expressions in it much relied on by the plaintiff, to show that the common law remedy was designed to remain, it is necessary to examine the statute somewhat in detail, to see whether there is any provision in it which cannot be reconciled with the apparent general intent of the legislature.

In the latter part of the second section, it is provided that the verdict of the jury, returned and allowed, shall be a sufficient bar to any action to be brought for damages; from which it is inferred, by the counsel for the plaintiff, that, *until* there is a verdict upon the process established by the statute, the common law remedy is open. But this construction would lead to a manifest absurdity. The statute was made for the relief of mill owners from a multiplicity of suits; still, however, it is left, upon this construction, to the party complaining of injury, to apply or withhold this remedy, as he shall choose. For the mill owner cannot commence this statute process; and he must therefore answer continually to actions brought against him, because his litigious adversary does not choose to have the controversy settled by the method prescribed in the statute. The expression relied upon in this section of the statute could intend nothing more than that the verdict returned, etc., should be final and conclusive between the parties, until the measures afterwards prescribed, to obtain an increase or decrease of the damages, should be resorted to by one of the parties.

It is also said that the statute does not provide for the assessment of any damages happening before the institution of the process, this remedy being altogether prospective. But we are satisfied that this is not the true construction of the act. The jury are to ascertain the yearly damages *done* to the complainant, and the process is given only to those who have actually suffered damage; so that the verdict is to be returned for the amount of damages already incurred; and the practice, in those counties where the remedy under the statute is in most frequent use, is conformable to this construction. I may say, also, that, in those counties, since the passing of this act, the common law action has gone entirely out of use, from a belief, as I apprehend, that it was superseded by the statute. But, further, in the third section of the statute, a new and independent provision is enacted, that the same verdict and judgment thereon shall be the measure of yearly damages for the future. Now, if the provision in the second section was merely prospective, it is not conceivable, however inartificially the statute may have been framed, that it would be immediately followed by another section, enacting over again the same thing in form and substance.

The fourth section of the statute may be recurred to, as removing all doubt as to the intention of the legislature to establish this process, as the only legal remedy for this species of injury.

It provides that, if the owners of mills shall refuse to give security to the complainant for the yearly damages which may have been ascertained, he shall have *no benefit of the act,* but shall be liable to be sued for flowing the lands of the complainant, in the same manner as if the act had not passed. This section recognizes the act as intended for the benefit of the mill owner; and it surely could not be for his benefit, he having no means of enforcing it, if it were left optional with the other party, to proceed under the act, or at common law, as if the act had not passed.

The latter clause of the same section provides that, if the mill owner shall flow lands at that season of the year which has been determined by the jury to be unsuitable, such flowing shall not be justified; more than intimating that the flowing of the lands at another season is justified, except under circumstances prohibited by the act. If justified or authorized by an act of the legislature, surely it cannot be a legal foundation for an action founded on tort.

It has been urged, by the counsel for the plaintiff, that this remedy is merely cumulative, leaving the common law remedy in full force. But so to consider it would be to defeat the manifest object of the legislature; which was not to give a new and additional remedy to the party injured, but to establish a right in the party causing the injury, subject only to a mode of indemnification which was supposed to be more convenient than the one before existing; because the use of the property, in the manner which causes the injury, is supposed to be of public importance.

I cannot help thinking that this statute was incautiously copied from the ancient colonial and provincial acts, which were passed when the use of mills, from the scarcity of them, bore a much greater value, compared to the land used for the purposes of agriculture, than at present. But with this we have nothing to do. As the law is, so we must declare it. And we are all of opinion that judgment cannot be entered in the action now under consideration, for the cause shown in the motion in arrest, and that the entry be, that the plaintiff take nothing by his writ.

16. Clark v. Foot (1811)*

Clark v. Foot *shows how the doctrine of negligence invaded traditional property values even where an "inherently dangerous" force, such as fire, was the cause of the harm. What made the negligence standard, as applied in this case, particularly onerous for injured parties was that the burden of proof was on the plaintiff. Since evidence of negligence, in most instances, was more likely to be under the control of the defendant, plaintiffs were confronted with the often insurmountable procedural difficulty of rounding up sufficient facts to persuade a jury. In* Clark v. Foot, *the only evidence on the negligence issue was produced by the defendant. Witnesses testified that the defendant had done what he could to contain the fire. Plaintiff could not show that the defendant was negligent. But under a strict liability regime, all Clark would have had to show in order to recover was that Foot started a fire that damaged Clark's property.*

Clark sued *Foot* before the justice, to recover damages sustained by reason of *Foot*'s setting fire to the plaintiff's woods.

The cause was tried by a jury. A witness testified that he set fire, by the direction of the defendant, to certain fallow ground, belonging to the defendant, which fire run [sic] into the woodlands of the plaintiff; that he told the defendant of it, who tried only to prevent the fire from burning his own farm. The fire burnt during six or seven days, on the pine hill of the plaintiff, and damaged his woodland to the amount of sixty dollars.

The return [i.e. record] stated that the defendant produced a number of witnesses, who testified nothing contradicting the materiality of the above evidence, and that the jury found a verdict for the defendant, on which the justice gave judgment.

* *Clark v. Foot,* 8 Johns. 421 (N.Y. 1811).

For further reading: Gary T. Schwartz, "Tort Law and the Economy in Nineteenth-Century America: A Reinterpretation," *Yale Law Journal,* vol. 90, (1981), 1717-1775.

Per Curiam. The point to be tried was, whether there was negligence on the part of *Foot,* or his agent; for *Foot* was as much accountable for the negligence of this servant, whilst employed in his business, as if the fire had spread by his own neglect.

It is a lawful act for a person to burn his fallow; and if his neighbor is injured thereby, he will have a remedy, by action on the case,* if there be sufficient ground to impute the act to the negligence or misconduct of the defendant or his servants.

Should a man's house get on fire, without his neglect, or default, and burn his neighbor's, no action would lie against him, notwithstanding the fire originated in his house, because it was lawful for him to keep fire there.... The same rule would apply to this case.

Here there is no evidence of negligence, and the jury have passed on the case.

Judgment affirmed.

17. *Fletcher v. Peck (1810)*†

While Marbury v. Madison *(Document 8) is the most famous Supreme Court case ever decided, its significance was not completely apparent at first. In fact, no other act of Congress was declared unconstitutional until the Dred Scott decision in 1857. More important, however, for the development of the constitutional system was the Court's assertion of its power to declare acts of state legislatures null and void. In* Fletcher v. Peck, *the question presented was whether or not a Georgia legislative land grant, passed by means of fraud, could be annulled by a subsequent legislature. In considering this question Marshall, speaking for a unanimous Supreme Court, held that the legislative grant was a contract, and that rights of property which had vested under that contractual grant could not be divested by a subsequent legislative act. To allow such divestment would violate the contract clause of the U.S. Constitution. Hence the second act of the Georgia legislature, the act of rescission, could have no legal effect.*

---

* "On the case" was a form of action for injury or loss that was done unintentionally, without the use of force, and where the damages were an indirect consequence of the defendant's behavior. An "action on the case" was also often used in suits against defendants whose agents actually performed the act causing the injury or loss, as here in *Clark v. Foot.*

† 10 U.S. (6 Cranch) 87 (1810). Available in Commager, *Documents of American History,* vol. 1.

For further reading: Alexander Bickel, *The Least Dangerous Branch: The Supreme Court at the Bar of Politics* (New York, 1962), chap. 1.

Justice Oliver Wendell Holmes, Jr., once remarked that the power of the Supreme Court to declare the acts of Congress unconstitutional was not critical. But, said Holmes, should the Supreme Court lose the power to review the constitutionality of state laws, the federal system would collapse. Why did Holmes make this distinction? Was his observation valid? Which interests did Marshall strengthen in Fletcher v. Peck *and which was he attempting to weaken? What would be the basis for a counterargument against Marshall's use of the contract clause in this case?*

MARSHALL, C.J.

The case, as made out in the pleadings, is simply this: One individual who holds lands in the state of Georgia, under a deed covenanting that the title of Georgia was in the grantor, brings an action of covenant upon this deed and assigns, as a breach, that some of the members of the legislature were induced to vote in favor of the law, which constituted the contract, by being promised an interest in it, and that, therefore, the act is a mere nullity.... If the title be plainly deduced from a legislative act, which the legislature might constitutionally pass, if the act be clothed with all the requisite forms of a law, a court, sitting as a court of law, cannot sustain a suit brought by one individual against another, founded on the allegation that the act is a nullity, in consequence of the impure motives which influenced certain members of the legislature which passed the law....

In this case, the legislature may have had ample proof that the original grant was obtained by practices which can never be too much reprobated, and which would have justified its abrogation, so far as respected those to whom crime was imputable. But the grant, when issued, conveyed an estate in fee-simple to the grantee, clothed with all the solemnities which law can bestow. This estate was transferrible; and those who purchased parts of it were not stained by that guilt which infected the original transaction....

Is the power of the legislature competent to the annihilation of such title, and to a resumption of the property thus held? The principle asserted is, that one legislature is competent to repeal any act which a former legislature was competent to pass; and that one legislature cannot abridge the powers of a succeeding legislature. The correctness of this principle, so far as respects general legislation, can never be controverted. But if an act be done under a law, a succeeding legislature cannot undo it. The past cannot be recalled by the most absolute power. Conveyances have been made, those conveyances have vested legal estates, and, if those estates may be seized by the sovereign authority, still, that they originally vested is a fact, and cannot cease to be a fact. When, then, a law is in its nature a contract, when absolute rights have vested under that contract, a repeal of the law cannot divest those rights; and the act of annulling them, if legitimate, is rendered so by a power applicable to the case of every individual in the community. . . .

The validity of this rescinding act, then, might well be doubted, were Georgia a single sovereign power. But Georgia cannot be viewed as a single, unconnected, sovereign power, on whose legislature no other restrictions are imposed than may be found in its own constitution. She is a part of a large empire; she is a member of the American union; and that union has a constitution, the supremacy of which all acknowledge, and which imposes limits to the legislatures of the several states, which none claim a right to pass. The constitution of the United States declares that no state shall pass any bill of attainder, *ex post facto law,* or law impairing the obligation of contracts.

Does the case now under consideration come within this prohibitory section of the Constitution? . . .

If, under a fair construction of the constitution, grants are comprehended under the term contracts, is a grant from the state excluded from the operation of the provision? Is the clause to be considered as inhibiting the state from impairing the obligation of contracts between two individuals, but as excluding from that inhibition contracts made with itself? The words themselves contain no such distinction. They are general, and are applicable to contracts of every description. If contracts made with the state are to be exempted from their operation, the exception must arise from the character of the contracting party, not from the words which are employed. . . .

It is, then, the unanimous opinion of the court, that, in this case, the estate having passed into the hands of a purchaser for a valuable consideration, without notice, the state of Georgia was restrained, either by general principles which are common to our free institutions, or by the particular provisions of the constitution of the United States, from passing a law whereby the estate of the plaintiff in the premises so purchased could be constitutionally and legally impaired and rendered null and void. . . .

18. Trial of the Philadelphia Cordwainers (1806)*

These excerpts from the three-day trial of the Philadelphia cordwainers focus on the interrelationship between the criminal conspiracy charges brought against these early trade unionists and underlying doctrines of political economy. While the prosecution likened this early labor union to a state within the state and declared it to be a threat to the liberties of all, the defense drew a parallel between this association of working people and other private associations organized for benevolent purposes. Indeed, the defense even used an extract from Adam Smith's Wealth of Nations *to argue its point of view. Which side, the prosecution or the defense, made the strongest argument? Is there any justification for the highly one-sided instruction the Court gave as its charge to the jury?*

[ARGUMENT BY THE PROSECUTION]

Let it be well understood that the present action, is not intended to introduce the doctrine, that a man is not at liberty to fix any price whatsoever upon his own labour; we disclaim the idea, in the most unqualified terms, we declare that every man, has a right to fix any price upon his commodities or his labour which he deems proper. We have no design to prevent him. We disclaim any such design. If any one of the defendants, had thought proper to charge $100 for making a pair of boots, nobody would interfere, if he could get his employer to give it, or could compel the payment. He would have a legal right to do so, our complaint is not of that kind. . . .

Our position is, that no man is at liberty to combine, conspire, confederate, and unlawfully agree to regulate the whole body of workmen in the city. The defendants are not indicted for regulating their own individual wages, but for undertaking by a combination, to regulate the price of the labour of others as well as their own. . . .

You will also please to observe that this body of journeymen are not an incorporated society whatever may have been represented out of doors on that head; neither are they a society instituted for benevolent purposes. But merely a society for compelling by the most arbitrary and

* *Commonwealth v. Pullis.* Source: *The Trial of the Boot and Shoemakers of Philadelphia, on an Indictment for a Combination and Conspiracy to Raise Their Wages* (Philadelphia, 1806). Available in John R. Commons et al., (eds.), *A Documentary History of American Industrial Society* (10 vols., New York, 1958), Vol. 3.

For further reading: Walter Nelles, "The First American Labor Case," *Yale Law Journal,* 41 (1931) 165–200.

malignant means, the whole body of the journeymen to submit to their rules and regulations; it is not confined even to the members of the society, it reaches every individual of the trade, whether journeyman or master. It will appear, from the evidence to be adduced before you, to spread to an extent of which you cannot as yet form any idea. You will find that they not only determine the price of labour for themselves, but compel every one to demand that price and receive no other, they refuse to hold communion with any person who shall disobey there mandates, in fine, they regulate the whole trade under the most dreadful pains and penalties, such I believe as never was heard of in this or any other civilized country....

This is the chief charge in the indictment; and you now see that the action is instituted to maintain the cause of liberty and repress that of licentiousness. It is to secure the rights of each individual to obtain and enjoy the price he fixes upon his own labour....

Why a combination in such case is criminal, will not be difficult to explain: we live under a government composed of a constitution and laws.... and every man is obliged to obey the constitution, and the laws made under it. When I say he is bound to obey these, I mean to state the whole extent of his obedience. Do you feel yourselves bound to obey any other laws, enacted by any other legislature, than that of your own choice? Shall these, or any other body of men, associate for the purpose of making new laws, laws not made under the constitutional authority, and compel their fellow citizens to obey them, under the penalty of their existence? This prosecution contravenes no man's right, it is to prevent an infringement of right; it is in favour of the equal liberty of all men, this is the policy of our laws; but if private associations and clubs, can make constitutions and laws for us ... if they can associate and make bye-laws paramount, or inconsistent with the state laws What, I ask, becomes of the liberty of the people, about which so much is prated; about which the opening counsel made such a flourish! ...

[ARGUMENT OF DEFENSE COUNSEL]

Now, if any journeyman who chose to work at the rates or prices offered by the employers, contrary to the wish of other journeymen, were threatened by them, or any of them, with injury to his person or property, he has a complete and ample remedy provided for him by law without resorting to the measures which have been adopted. He might have them bound over to their good behaviour, and if they afterwards were guilty of any threats, their recognizance would be forfeited, and they would be obliged to pay the penalty. But it does not appear that either of the defendants or members of that association, uttered any menaces or were guilty of any assault. Blair said, some of his people were beaten, in 1799, but that is not brought home to either of the defendants.

If any employer suffer inconvenience or mischief, in consequence of his journeymen being seduced or driven from his employment, he has his remedy by a civil action, in which he may recover from the offender, damages equal to the injury sustained. These points are made to show, that these employers are not without their remedy....

Is there the slightest evidence, that the defendants ever compelled a single journeyman to leave his employer? How did they compel? Did they use any violence? If they had they were subject to the laws and might have been individually punished for it. But neither violence, threats, nor menaces, were used.... No man was the object of force or compulsion.... "The very head and front of their offending was" their refusing to work for any master who employed such journeymen as infringed the rules of the society to which they belonged.

This I deny to be an offence. There is no crime in my refusing to work with a man who is not of the same association with myself. Supposing the ground of my refusal to be ever so unreasonable or ridiculous...to be in reality, mere caprice or whim.... Still it is no crime.... The motive for my refusal may be illiberal, but it furnishes no legal foundation for a prosecution: I cannot be indicted for it. Every man may chuse his company, or refuse to associate with any one whose company may be disagreeable to him, without being obliged to give a reason for it: and without violating the laws of the land....

I will conclude this part of my argument, with the remarks of a very sensible and judicious writer, which are so apposite to the subject before you, that I think it right to submit them to your consideration. 1. Smith's *Wealth of Nations,* page 89.

> Workmen desire to get as much, masters to give as little, as possible. The former are disposed to combine in order to raise, the latter in order to lower. It is not, however, difficult to foresee which of the two parties must, upon all ordinary occasions, have the advantage in the dispute, and force the other into a compliance with their terms. The masters being fewer in number, can combine much more easily; and the law, besides, authorises, or at least does not prohibit their combinations, while it prohibits those of the workmen. We have no acts of parliament against combining to lower the price of work;

but many against combining to raise it. In all such disputes the masters can hold out much longer. A landlord, a farmer, a master manufacturer, or merchant, though they did not employ a single workman, could generally live a year or two upon the stocks which they have already acquired. Many workmen could not subsist a week, few could subsist a month, and scarce any a year without employment. In the long run the workman may be as necessary to his master, as his master is to him; but the necessity is not so immediate. We rarely hear, it has been said, of the combinations of masters; though frequently of those of workmen. But whoever imagines, upon this account, that masters rarely combine, is as ignorant of the world as the subject. Masters are always and every where in a sort of tacit, but constant and uniform combination, not to raise the wages of labour above their actual rate. To violate this combination is every where a most unpopular action, and a sort of reproach to a master among his neighbours and equals. We seldom, indeed, hear of this combination, because it is the usual, and one may say, the natural state of things, which nobody ever hears of. Masters too, sometimes enter into particular combinations to sink the wages of labour below this rate. These are always conducted with the utmost silence and secrecy, till the moment of execution, and when the workmen yield, as they sometimes do, without resistance, though severely felt by them, they are never heard of by other people.

If you are desirous of introducing a similar spirit of inequality into our government and laws . . . if you think that the labourer and the journeyman enjoy too great a portion of liberty, and ought to be restricted in their rights . . . such disposition and opinions will lead you to convict the defendants. If, on the other hand, you are satisfied with the wise and liberal principles of our government . . . if you are contented with the blessings enjoyed under our free constitution, which secures to the citizens an equality of rights, and recognizes no distinction of classes . . . I shall look for the result of these feelings and these sentiments in a verdict of acquittal.

[THE COURT'S CHARGE TO THE JURY]

What is the case now before us? . . . A combination of workmen to raise their wages may be considered in a two fold point of view: one is to benefit themselves . . . the other is to injure those who do not join their society. The rule of law condemns both. If the rule be clear, we are bound to conform to it even though we do not comprehend the principle upon which it is founded. We are not to reject it because we do not see the reason of it. It is enough, that it is the will of the majority. It is law because it is their will—if it is law, there may be good reasons for it though we cannot find them out. But the rule in this case is pregnant with sound sense and all the authorities are clear upon the subject. Hawkins, the greatest authority on the criminal law, has laid it down, that a combination to maintaining one another, carrying a particular object, whether true or false, is criminal. . . . Is this like the formation of a society for the promotion of the general welfare of the community, such as to advance the interests of religion, or to accomplish acts of charity and benevolence? Is it like the society for extinguishing fires? or those for the promotion of literature and the fine arts, or the meeting of the city wards to nominate candidates for the legislature or the executive? These are for the benefit of third persons the society in question to promote the selfish purposes of the members. The mere mention of them is an answer to all, that has been said on that point. There is no comparison between the two; they are as distinct as light and darkness. How can these cases be considered on an equal footing? . . .

These sentiments of the court, not an individual of which is connected either with the masters or journeymen; all stand independent of both parties . . . are unanimous. They have given you the rule as they have found it in the book, and it is now for you to say, whether the defendants are guilty or not. The rule they consider as fixed, they cannot change it. It is now, therefore, left to you upon the law, and the evidence to find the verdict. If you can reconcile it to your consciences, to find the defendants not guilty, you will do so; if not, the alternative that remains, is a verdict of guilty.

[THE JURY VERDICT]

The reporter took it down in these words: We find the defendants guilty of a combination to raise their wages, Subscribed by the 12 jurors. . . .

And the court fined the defendants eight dollars each, with costs of suit, and to stand committed till paid.

The Batture
Controversy:
A Case Study in
Early Nineteenth-
Century Legal
History

Introduction

The controversy over the alluvial land known as the New Orleans
Batture was one of the most explosive of the early nineteenth century. It
began as a local dispute between private parties and the people of the
city of New Orleans, but before very long it involved the national
government, including the President of the United States. Litigation
over the Batture continued for many years. Some of it even reached the
United States Supreme Court. The controversy generated great bodies
of legal documentation as the parties of interest, both public and
private, pressed their claims in various forums and in a variety of ways.
As a result, a rich assortment of historical material exists, illustrating the
multiplicity of sources that need to be consulted in order to reconstruct

the events surrounding this unique and interesting dispute. Besides the court papers that the Batture cases produced there are legal briefs, affidavits and depositions, correspondence over legal strategy, legislative statutes, addresses to the public, and editorial comment in newspapers—all of which illuminate different aspects of the public debate over the disposition of the Batture grounds.

The Batture controversy is a good example of the relationship between law and politics in American history. Its political and social ramifications were of such magnitude that they exceeded the ability of the judicial system to handle it. This was the most important oversight committed by the private parties to the original lawsuit. And in this they have not been alone, for throughout American history, and even today, there is an expectation, often incapable of realization, that courts of law are the proper forum for resolving deep social issues. These expectations are based on the theory that courts are neutral bodies whose only task is to apply a fixed body of law to a fluid social situation and thereby resolve difficult issues in an objective and fair-minded manner. The fact is, however, that much of law is not fixed or neutral but open-ended, value-laden, and "plastic" as Jefferson called it. The effort to escape politics through law is, therefore, often a fruitless one. The larger the social ramifications of a legal dispute, the less likely it is that an attempt to resolve the issue by judicial means will succeed.

Outline of the Controversy

OVERVIEW OF THE CASE

Each year the Mississippi River deposits rich layers of alluvial sediment along its banks. In Louisiana this alluvion is called *batture*.[1] The Batture Ste. Marie was located between the New Orleans suburb (or faubourg) of that name and the river. The suburb had originally been part of a land grant owned by the Jesuits; but after the Jesuit order was expelled from Louisiana in the 1760s, title to the Batture passed by successive transfers to one Bertrand Gravier in 1785. Gravier established

---

[1] The word batture is equivalent to the common-law term for land formed by accretion. It is derived from the French verb *se battre* (to beat) since the *batture* is that place where the water beats against the shore and deposits alluvion in the process.

suburban lots on the old Jesuit land grant, some of which he sold in the 1790s.

At issue was whether or not the *batture* adjacent to the suburb belonged to Gravier, to the suburban lot grantees, or to the public at large. The people of New Orleans customarily used *batture* soil to fill in streets and sidewalks, and to shore up the levee against seasonal overflows of the Mississippi River. Jean Gravier, the heir of Bertrand, began to make improvements on the Batture in 1803. Perhaps in anticipation of its growing commercial potential as a wharfage area, he attempted to stop the local residents of the city from coming onto the site in order to use it in the usual manner. Consequently Gravier brought a lawsuit to establish his title to the Batture and to block further intrusions by the local inhabitants. After several continuances, the case was decided in his favor in May 1807.

John Gravier's principal attorney was Edward Livingston, a well-known Jeffersonian Democrat, a former mayor of New York City, and a recent "immigrant" to Louisiana from New York. Because of personal indebtedness Livingston was in need of capital, and he quickly saw the value of the Batture in the economic life of the entire Mississippi Basin. He acquired an interest in the property, some said in payment for the legal services he rendered to Jean Gravier. Livingston thereupon commenced improvements of his own on the property. This precipitated a series of violent confrontations between Livingston's workmen and the people of New Orleans. The municipality, in cooperation with territorial authorities, transferred its alleged title to the Batture to the United States government—on the theory that the Batture, having once belonged to France, had passed to the United States by right of succession as sovereign in Louisiana. By the fall of 1807 the national administration in Washington was being called upon to take decisive action in New Orleans.

Satisfied that the legal claims of the public were superior to those of Gravier or Livingston, the Jefferson administration ordered the U.S. marshal in New Orleans to evict Livingston as an intruder on public land, pursuant to an act of Congress passed on March 3, 1807. Livingston appealed directly to the President and then to Congress but without success. Then, in separate actions, he filed suit against the marshal in New Orleans and, in 1810, against Thomas Jefferson, then retired from office, in Richmond, Virginia. Livingston would eventually lose in his litigation with the former President, but not before a great deal of political maneuvering and manipulation of appointments to the federal bench had taken place. Livingston did succeed in his suit against the marshal in New Orleans, however, although many years would pass before he would realize any tangible benefits from his considerable personal investment in the Batture.

THE BATTURE AND THE LAW

On October 22, 1805, John Gravier petitioned the Superior Court of the Orleans Territory (Lower Louisiana) for damages resulting from the repeated trespasses by the inhabitants of New Orleans on the Batture Ste. Marie, which he claimed as private property. (See pp. 116–117.) He also sought a decree that would quiet his title to the property. On December 18, 1805, the court issued a preliminary injunction temporarily barring the inhabitants from digging in the Batture or carrying away any of its soil except for emergency repairs of the levee, pending a trial of the action on the merits. Early in 1807 the case was tried by a panel of three judges. The defendants could have had a jury trial of the action, but perhaps because of their lack of familiarity with this procedure of Anglo-American common law they chose to have a bench trial— undoubtedly to the delight of the plaintiff's attorneys. Significantly, all four of the plaintiff's lawyers had English or American surnames, while two of the three attorneys representing the city were French. (See p. 117.)

On May 23, 1807, the superior court rendered its decision. (See pp. 118–119.) The court made the following findings of fact: (1) that the Batture had already formed at the time Bertrand Gravier acquired possession of the faubourg St. Marie in the 1780s; (2) that the Batture was then of sufficient height to be considered separate property; (3) that the Batture and the faubourg were bounded by the river; and (4) that Bertrand Gravier had not abandoned the Batture after he had divided the faubourg and sold off lots in it. As a matter of law, the court determined that since the defendants had no prescriptive rights[2] in the property, title to the Batture had not passed to the city or to its inhabitants but remained in Bertrand Gravier and his lawful successor in interest, namely Jean Gravier. Accordingly, the court granted the plaintiff's petition that he be quieted in his possession, and it perma-

---

[2] In Louisiana *prescription* means the acquisition of land through long, continuous, and open use adverse to the proprietary interest of the true owner over a period of years fixed by law. It is similar to the common-law doctrine known as *adverse possession*.

nently enjoined the defendants from interfering with his private enjoyment of the Batture property.

In arriving at its decision, the superior court applied Spanish law rather than French law to the facts in dispute. Under Spanish law, alluvial deposits bordering navigable streams, such as the Mississippi, belonged to the riparian owner. In contrast, under French law such deposits were part of the bed of the river and belonged to the public or to the sovereign. Thereafter, the issue as to whether or not the court had applied the correct body of law (Spanish rather than French) was hotly contested. Those who favored Gravier, Livingston, and the right of private ownership supported the court and its application of Spanish law; those who supported the public's claim argued that the court had erred and that French law applied. Given the overwhelmingly French orientation of the population, this aspect of the decision inflamed public opinion. The fact that the three judges who decided the case were all recent immigrants from the United States made the new American regime extremely unpopular in Lower Louisiana. The policy the Jefferson administration subsequently devised for dealing with the Batture problem can be understood, in large measure, as an effort to combat this unpopularity.

POLICY DECISIONS BY THE FEDERAL GOVERNMENT

In the aftermath of the court's decision, the advocates for the city of New Orleans began to gather evidence to support a petition to Congress to defend the public's right to the Batture. In the fall of 1807, one Jean Baptiste Macarty was chosen to make a personal representation to the government in Washington, D.C. Macarty collected affidavits and depositions attesting to long and uninterrupted public usage of the Batture and the abandonment of the property by the Graviers. (See pp. 121–123.) These depositions helped to build a case to support the theory that the United States was the rightful owner of the Batture by right of succession to the entire territory of Louisiana.

The superior court's decision in the Batture case had policy implications quite at odds with the two political branches of the federal government. By the act of March 3, 1807, Congress had authorized the forcible removal of squatters from public lands. (See pp. 123–124.) This act provided the statutory underpinnings for the order sent to the U.S. marshal in New Orleans to remove Livingston from the Batture. (See p. 125.) Jefferson had ordered this action on the basis of an advisory opinion from Attorney General Caesar Rodney. (See pp. 124–125.) Rodney considered Livingston to be in violation of the act. Livingston would argue that he was not an intruder on public land but a good faith purchaser who took possession directly from Jean Gravier, whose title to the Batture had been upheld by the Superior Court of Orleans. Livingston would also challenge the constitutionality of the antisquatter statute, since it authorized the use of military force rather than judicial process to evict a holder in peaceable possession and thus gave to the President powers in excess of those delegated to him under the Constitution.

After ordering the removal of Livingston and his workers from the Batture, Jefferson put the case before Congress. (See p. 126.) There the issue was debated for the next two years, from 1808 to 1810, only to die in the end. But while the Batture was under consideration, all of the major parties to the dispute pushed for a favorable outcome. The Orleans territorial legislature even instructed its delegate in Congress, a nonvoting observer who was privileged to speak, to press the claims of the public to the Batture. (See pp. 127–128.)

LIVINGSTON AGAINST JEFFERSON

Livingston was indefatigable in his own behalf. (See pp. 128–129.) And even from retirement, Jefferson himself was not above using his political influence to have Congress act in ways that would vindicate policy decisions on the Batture taken while he was still President. The ex-President orchestrated a plan that would short-circuit any Congressional action that might have an effect on the lawsuit that Livingston filed against him in federal court in Virginia early in 1810.[3]

Livingston alleged that Jefferson had used illegal force to evict him from the Batture and that, in effect, Jefferson had trespassed on Livingston's private property. Jefferson, a lawyer by profession, planned his own defense strategy. He also sought the aid of the leaders of the Virginia bar, but despite their advice that he try for a decision on the merits of the case, the former President preferred to win, if he could, on a procedural technicality. At Jefferson's insistence, therefore, his attorneys entered a special plea (called a plea in abatement), which challenged the jurisdiction of the Virginia court to try an action for a

[3] The principal reason why Livingston chose to sue Jefferson in Virginia rather than in Louisiana was because a Louisiana court would have lacked "personal jurisdiction" over the ex-President.

trespass to land situated in Louisiana. Jefferson also used his substantial influence among leading Republicans to block any action in Congress that might favor Livingston. (See pp. 129–130.) He justified his blandishments on the grounds that such action would be prejudicial to a "fair trial" on the merits of Livingston's claim, even while he actively pursued a litigation strategy that would defeat any possibility of such a trial.[4]

Finally, to assure a favorable outcome of that litigation, Jefferson pressured his successor in office, James Madison, to make several appointments to the federal bench that were likely to benefit Jefferson's defense. (See pp. 130–131.) Cyrus Griffin, an old Federalist judge on the Federal Circuit Court for the Virginia district, was ailing. Jefferson urged Madison to appoint former Virginia governor John Tyler to the vacancy. In addition, in September 1810, United States Supreme Court Justice William Cushing died, leaving the Court divided between three Federalists and three Republicans. This was the first real opportunity since the election of 1800 to create a Republican majority on the Court, but the former President's concern was as much personal as it was political. Should Livingston prevail in federal court in Virginia, Jefferson planned to appeal to the Supreme Court of the United States, and he was not above making an attempt to guarantee that the Supreme Court would be friendly. (See pp. 131–134.)

Since Cushing was from New England, his replacement would also have to be from that part of the country. But Jefferson was suspicious of all New Englanders—Republicans and Federalists alike. Like many southerners, he believed New England was steeped in Calvinist dogma and Puritan provincialism. New England's opposition in 1808 to Jefferson's Embargo policy still rankled with him. Levi Lincoln, a former attorney general, was Jefferson's first choice, but Lincoln declined because of failing eyesight. Others considered for the post included Postmaster General Gideon Granger and John Quincy Adams, then ambassador to Russia. Eventually, Madison chose Joseph Story although Jefferson suspected, rightly as it happens, that Story was philosophically closer to the Federalist party and was only nominally a Jeffersonian in his politics.

---

[4] Jefferson also claimed that, as a former president, he should be immune from suit for an action taken in his official capacity. Not until 1982, however, did the Supreme Court recognize such a doctrine of absolute presidential immunity from civil suits. See *Nixon v. Fitzgerald*, 50 U.S.L.W. 4797 (June 24, 1982).

Jefferson's confidence in Tyler was not misplaced, nor was his litigation strategy misdirected. Late in 1811, the Virginia Circuit Court dismissed Livingston's suit. (See pp. 134–136.) "It seems clear then," wrote the newly appointed Tyler, "that...where title of land is in question, the action must be local....Upon the ground taken, so far then, the action cannot be maintained in this court." Chief Justice John Marshall, the other judge of the circuit court,[5] concurred, but he could not resist the chance to criticize Jefferson for avoiding a decision on the merits. He wrote in his opinion that the alleged trespasser, namely Jefferson, was "amenable to the court of that district [Orleans] in which the land lies, and in which he will never be found."[6]

Thus Jefferson's efforts to thwart Livingston succeeded at every turn. He managed to block him in all three branches of the federal government. First, as President, Jefferson had Livingston physically removed from the Batture. Subsequently, even after his retirement from the presidency, Jefferson exercised his extraordinary political influence to frustrate Livingston both in Congress and in the federal courts. It was an adroit display of Jefferson's political talents and a demonstration of how political power can overcome the separation among the three branches of government. Indeed, Livingston never fully realized that a winning political strategy was ultimately more important to the outcome of the Batture dispute than even the best-researched legal brief.

SUMMARY AND CONCLUSION

In retrospect, the Batture controversy is a minor episode in a period when great events crowded in on one another. It occurred at a time when the nation was beset with growing international tensions that would eventually lead to war with Great Britain. The Batture dispute ripened at a time when Jefferson's dramatic policy of "peaceful coercion" in the

---

[5] For well over a century, Supreme Court justices were required to "ride the circuit" in order to hear cases and appeals in the federal circuit courts. By the 1830s some of the justices were logging thousands of miles annually. At least one nominee to the office declined appointment because of this arduous burden. Not until 1911 was circuit-riding ended by statute. See Felix Frankfurter and James M. Landis, *The Business of the Supreme Court: A Study in the Federal Judicial System* (New York, 1928), chap. 1.

[6] The case of *Livingston v. Jefferson* has remained a landmark case in the law of civil procedure. It stands for the proposition that an action for trespass to land is "local" and not "transitory," which means that it must be brought in the state where the land lies. Despite the fact that they were distant cousins, or perhaps because of it, Jefferson and Marshall had a long-standing personal and political feud. For further discussion, see Francis N. Stites, *John Marshall: Defender of the Constitution* (Boston, 1981).

form of the Embargo Act was just beginning to take effect. In short, the Batture dispute and the policy decisions taken with respect to it, although interesting, was a problem of decidedly secondary importance to Jefferson's final term in office.

Nevertheless, the facts and ideas connected with the Batture problem touched basic historical issues and themes that continued to resonate and reverberate in later years. For these reasons, the Batture controversy opens a small window onto the American past. Clearly, a major part of the dispute, and an important reason why there was such agitation over it in the locality most affected, was the way in which a vital public resource, the alluvial lands adjacent to New Orleans, was transferred from public to private control. The public perceived the decisions of the territorial court and the subsequent proprietary activities of Edward Livingston as a transfer of valuable public domain to private hands with apparent disregard for the public interest.

In addition, the position taken by Jefferson on the Batture issue does not reflect any clear consistency with positions he had taken earlier as Washington's secretary of state and then as Vice President in the administration of John Adams. Having been closely identified with opposition to the assertion of federal power in economic affairs over such issues as the national debt, internal improvements, and the Bank of the United States, and having been a staunch defender of a free press at the time of the Alien and Sedition Laws, Jefferson assumed more of a Hamiltonian posture in the Batture dispute. He sided with government against private interests and was attacked by Livingston as an enemy of civil liberties and constitutional due process.

Viewed in an even larger historical perspective, the transfer of the Batture to private control was not unique. Public policy in the nation's early history was committed to precisely this kind of resource allocation and development. Land was the most valuable resource at the government's disposal, but for at least two reasons it was thought desirable to put it in private hands rather than leave it as public domain. First, there was fear that undistributed land would greatly expand and dangerously enhance the government's wealth and power. Fear of excessive political dominion was a primary motivation in limiting the economic resources of the state at every level. Second, since government was small it was not in a position to develop the public domain as efficiently as private actors could. By placing landed resources in private hands, new sources of energy would be released. On a large scale this was best illustrated by the land distribution policy that developed out of the disposition of the

Northwest Territory in the 1780s. In the Land Ordinance of 1784, for example, public land was subdivided into lots in order to encourage small landowners to purchase at low cost. The Batture shows the same underlying philosophy at work. The law favored private over public usage and control. Thus Edward Livingston, on the authority of the superior court decision in *Gravier v. New Orleans,* undertook extensive engineering projects to enclose and improve the Batture while blocking the kind of casual usage to which the people of New Orleans were accustomed.

The theme of "privatization," then, which was a major trend in American legal history in the period following the American Revolution, is very much at the heart of the Batture dispute. Indeed, it is the central issue behind the political turmoil the case generated in the Territory of Orleans in the first decade of the nineteenth century.

Documents in the Batture Controversy

*John Gravier v. The Mayor, Aldermen, and inhabitants of the City of New Orleans**

PETITION OF JOHN GRAVIER

That [John Gravier] is the lawful owner of a certain parcel of land called the Batture, in front of the suburb St. Mary.

That the mayor, aldermen, and inhabitants of the city of New Orleans pretend to some right therein, and disturb the petitioner by publications tending to discredit his title, by trespasses in digging the earth, and lately by erecting a cabin thereon; by reason whereof persons who have contracted for the purchase of parts of this land refuse to pay, and the petitioner is endamaged to ten thousand dollars.

Praying that the mayor, etc., may set forth their title.

That he may be quieted in his possession.

And that he may receive such damages as the court may assess.

---

*Source: U.S. Congress, *American State Papers,* 38 vols, (Washington, D.C., 1789–1838), *Public Lands,* vol. 2, pp. 22–102.

ANSWER OF THE DEFENDANTS

The defendants now and at all times, etc. answer and say:

That they cannot admit that the petitioner has been at any time the owner of the parcel of land alluded to in his petition, if he meant by that the parcel commonly called the Batture, which lies between the levee and the river Mississippi, in the whole extent of the suburb St. Mary; they expressly deny that at any time this petitioner had any manner of possession of the same.

That the truth is, that some time before the death of Bertrand Gravier, the first owner of the plantation on the front of which the suburb St. Mary was established, he the said Bertrand Gravier had abandoned, and himself acknowledges, in an unequivocal manner, to have abandoned to the public all the above-mentioned parcel of land.

That in consequence of such abandonment, the highway and levee have been maintained and repaired then and afterwards till this moment, either by *corvées publiques* or at the expense of the city.

That since that time till now the inhabitants of this city never ceased to have a public and peaceful enjoyment of the said parcel, either to place different wood yards, or for unloading flat-bottomed boats and other rafts, which bring provisions to the city, with permission of the corporation.

That under the Spanish Government some individuals having undertaken to establish some buildings on the said parcel of land, contrary to the said enjoyment, the said buildings were immediately destroyed and pulled down by order of the Government.

That in consequence of the said enjoyment the city council has caused several months ago a cabin to be erected on the said tract of land, to lodge a guardian to take care of the same, and the earth thereof to be digged and carried away for the repair of the levee along the same.

Therefore your petitioners pray to be hence dismissed with costs.

[ARGUMENTS OF THE PETITIONER]

Counsel for the Plaintiff, Messrs. James Brown, Livingston, Duncan, Kerr, for the defendants, Messrs. Gurley, (attorney general,) Moreau, Derbigny.

The plaintiff's counsel in opening stated that the land now in dispute was an alluvion formed in front of the plantation now belonging to the plaintiff, and which had formerly made a part of the Jesuits' plantation adjoining the city of New Orleans. That he would show a title to, and actual possession of the farm, of which this alluvion formed a part, in the plaintiff and those under whom he claimed, ever since the year 1726. That of the alluvion itself he would show a constructive legal possession from the time it was first formed, and an actual possession from the time it became a sufficient height, extent, and value to justify the expense of improving it.

[ARGUMENTS OF THE DEFENDANTS]

[T]he defendants relied on the following points, which were not stated in the order they are here reported, but are collected from the arguments of the different counsel on the three several arguments. This method in stating them will be an advantage, that may in some measure compensate for the reporter's inability to do justice to the strength of manner and language with which the defense was conducted.

    I. That Bertrand Gravier had never had a title to the Batture.
    II. That John Gravier could not claim the Batture under the inventory, appraisement, and adjudication of Bertrand's property.
    III. That the city had a title to the land—
        1st. By the abandonment of Bertrand Gravier.
        2d. By the operation of law when the suburb was laid out.
        3d. By prescription as to the soil.
        4th. That they had a prescriptive right, if not to the property of the soil, at least to a servitude or commonable [sic] right to use it for digging earth and storing lumber, etc.

JUDGMENT OF THE SUPERIOR COURT OF THE TERRITORY OF ORLEANS

1st.   The title of Bertrand Gravier, the ancestor of the plaintiff, to the tract of land on which the faubourg St. Mary is situated has not been disputed; but it has been contended that this tract was bounded by the highway; the court, however, are of opinion that, according to the evidence exhibited, and the general usage of the country, this tract of land was bounded by the river Mississippi.

2d.   From the examination of the authorities, the court are of opinion that, according to the civil and Spanish laws, the right of alluvion is incident to land which is bounded by a navigable river, and that these laws must form the rule of decision in the present case.

3d. If Bertrand Gravier, therefore, had continued proprietor of the whole tract on which the faubourg has been established, there would be no difficulty in determining his title to the alluvion; but Bertrand Gravier had divested himself of all title to that part of his tract on which the faubourg is established by selling the lots fronting and adjoining the highway. It is therefore important to inquire, what was the situation of the Batture or alluvion in question, at the time the faubourg was established; or at least when the front lots were sold: For if no alluvion existed at that time, when Bertrand Gravier ceased to be the owner of the land adjourning the high road, then it is the opinion of the court that an alluvion subsequently formed would not become the property of Bertrand Gravier....

It is, however, the opinion of the court, from the evidence adduced in this cause, that, antecedent to the time when Bertrand Gravier ceased to be the proprietor of the land adjacent to the high road, a Batture or alluvion had been formed adjoining the levee, in front of the faubourg, upon the river; and that this alluvion was then of sufficient height to be considered as private property, and had consequently become annexed to, and incorporated with, the inheritance of Bertrand Gravier.

4th. Bertrand Gravier having then acquired, by alluvion, the property now in dispute, it is to be considered whether he has divested himself of his title to the same. The court are of opinion that he has not. The evidence of abandonment is merely conversation, which passed a long time ago; it is not very explicit and is much impaired by the circumstance of Bertrand Gravier having sold a part of his Batture to one of the front proprietors. It would be dangerous to divest a man of his property upon evidence of such declarations, without any proof of a consideration.

With respect to the claim of prescription, it is sufficient to observe that there has been no exclusive possession on the part of the defendants, and consequently they have no title on this ground. There are, indeed, other strong objections to a prescriptive title in this case, but the one we have stated is considered as sufficient.

5th. With respect to the title of John Gravier, as founded on the inventory, appraisement, and adjudication, which has been adduced in this cause, it is the opinion of the court that they are not bound to determine the validity or invalidity of this title. First, whether John Gravier has purchased the whole, or only inherited an undivided part, his claim to be quieted in the lawful enjoyment of the property in question, against the adverse pretensions of the city to the property of the soil, or the right of carrying it away, is sufficiently strong to enable the court to form a decision of the present case.

It is therefore ordered, adjudged, and decreed by the court, that the petitioner be quieted in his lawful enjoyment of the Batture, or alluvion, described in his petition, against the claims and pretensions of the defendants, and that the injunction heretofore granted in this case be made perpetual.

MOTION FOR A NEW TRIAL

After the judgment the defendants moved for a new trial, on the ground that the title was in the United States.

Newspaper Advertisement*

Earth and building sand for sale. All persons desirous of procuring EARTH or fine SAND for building, may be supplied by applying to CALALOU, Overseer of the works on the Batture, at the foot of Girod Street.

Edward Livingston

Ordinance of the City Council†

On the repeated complaints of many citizens, that they are obliged to buy the earth necessary for building and filling up their yards, and constructing their banquets, and that a great number of them have not even means adequate to this disbursement. The City Council considering that it is incumbent on them to bring some relief to the painful situation of the inhabitants of the city in this occurrence, RESOLVE, that notwithstanding the works already commenced by the corporation, and the... detriment by which the interests of the city and part of the commerce shall be affected, the mayor is provisionally authorized to cause, that earth from the Batture opposite fort St. Louis, be delivered

* *Le Telegraphe,* October 13, 1807. The *Telegraphe* was one of three French language newspapers in New Orleans during the territorial period. These newspapers accommodated their American readers by printing everything in English as well as in French.
† Ordinance of the New Orleans City Council, October 15, 1807. Available in City Council Records (New Orleans Public Library), vol. 2, bk. 1.

GRATIS, to all properties of lots and houses in town and fauxbourg St. Mary, who may be able to prove the indispensible necessity of this relief.

Charles Trudeau, President
James Mather, Mayor

Press Notice*

To the Public:

The illegal force which deprived me of the enjoyment of my property on the BATTURE of the Suburb St. Mary, having now ceased to operate—the late Marshal, the present Marshal, and the Attorney of the United States, having all declared under oath, in open Court, that they had no instructions from the Government relative to the said property—the claims of the City having been decided on, and the Mayor having lately declared on oath, that the Corporation were not in possession, and claimed not title thereto—I have peaceably, in the presence of several magistrates and other respectable witnesses, resumed the possession of my said property. And I hereby give notice that I permit all boats, flats and rafts, to load and unload on the said BATTURE, without paying any wharfage or any other charge whatever, and that the water-carts may fill at the accustomed places. But I will sue, without distinction every person who from henceforward shall dig the earth or committ any other trespass thereon.

Edward Livingston

Depositions†

...that of Andres Fernandez, [to the effect that] in the capacity of attorney to Joseph Rodulph Ducros, Depositor General, [he had been] ordered by the Court of the Auditor of War to take charge and possession of all the moveable and immoveable estate, lands, etc., of the

---

* *Louisiana Gazette,* November 17, 1810. The *Gazette* was one of the two major English language newspapers in New Orleans in the territorial period.

† Summaries of depositions taken by Colonel Jean Baptiste Macarty, October 1807, on behalf of the city of New Orleans. Source: Louisiana Miscellany, Manuscripts Division, Library of Congress.

estate of Bertrand Gravier and that according to the Inventory of said estate the Batture was never included in it.

...that of Pierre Rousseau, to the effect that the Batture was always for public use, for depositing wood thereon, or for taking earth for buildings, raising the courts-yards, repairing the streets and for discharging thereon the provisions of Barges, Pirogues, and Chalans.

...that of Francis Caisergnes, that he had been syndic procurator and alcalde under the Spanish, and a proprietor, that the Batture had always been public property, that proprietors who had erected buildings on the batture were obliged to throw them down by order of the Government; that requests to build on the batture such as that of Claude Girard were refused.

...that of Jayme Jorda, proprietor, Spanish member of the Cabildo, deposed that Batture was for public use and not for private profit, and that the policy of the Spanish government was to remove all erections on the Batture as encumbrances, for it served as a depot for loading and discharging goods of public necessity, also as a station for all boats, barges, pirogues, and flatboats, and the public might take earth for houses, lots, yards, and repair of streets.

...that of Mme. Francoise Trudeau, dweller on the levee of the suburb St. Mary, French, native of the city, deposes that the batture was always public property, that boats always unloaded there, that earth was always used for public use and the government always supplied criminals for the upkeep of the levy; that as a result of the fire of 1794, she and her mother rented a chalan to use as a house on the batture but they were forced off by both Governor Carondelet, and then by Gayoso.

...that of Jacques Livaudais, ancient commandant of the upper suburb of the city, native, deposes that the batture was always for public use, that the Spanish government ordered demolition of works on the batture, that under Carondelet, the public road between the faubourg and the batture was impassable and that B. Gravier denied responsibility to repair the same which he would have done by custom if the batture was his.

...that of Juan de Castenado, regidor under the Spanish government, deposes that Spanish governors repeatedly called for destruction of erections on the Batture; further, that galley slaves worked on the repairs of the Levee and the highway and that the Cabildo after the fire of 1794, presuming that the public wanted earth even at the time of the high water, caused a counter levee to be built so that the batture would not be inundated.

Act to Prevent Squatters*

Be it enacted by the Senate and House of Representatives of the United States of America in Congress assembled, That if any person or persons shall, after the passing of this act, take possession of, or make a settlement on any lands ceded or secured to the United States, by any treaty made with a foreign nation, or by a cession from any state to the United States,... which lands... shall not have been previously recognized and confirmed by the United States: or if any person or persons shall cause such lands to be thus occupied, taken possession of, or settled: or shall survey, or attempt to survey, or cause to be surveyed, any such lands; or designate any boundaries thereon, by marking trees, or otherwise, until thereto duly authorized by law; such offender or offenders, shall forfeit all his or their right, title, and claim, if any he hath, or they have, of whatsoever nature or kind the same shall or may be, to the lands aforesaid, which he or they shall have taken possession of, or settled,... or which he or they shall have surveyed, or attempt to survey, or cause to be surveyed, or the boundaries thereof he or they shall have designated, or cause to be designated, by marking trees or otherwise. And it shall moreover be lawful for the President of the United States, to direct the marshal, or officer acting as marshal, in the manner herein after directed, and also to take such other measures, and to employ such military force as he may judge necessary and proper, to remove from lands ceded, or secured to the United States, by treaty, or cession as aforesaid, any person or persons who shall hereafter take possession of the same, or make, or attempt to make a settlement thereon, until thereunto authorized by law. And every right, title, or

---

* An act to prevent settlements on lands ceded to the United States, until authorized by law. 9th Cong. 2d sess. Chap. 46, March 3, 1807. Source: U.S. Congress, *Statutes at Large,* Richard Peters (ed.), (Boston, 1856), vol. 2, pp. 445–446.

claim, forfeited under this act, shall be taken and deemed to be vested in the United States, without any other or further proceedings....

Sec. 2. *And be it further enacted,* That any person or persons who, before the passing of this act, had taken possession of, occupied, or made a settlement on any lands ceded or secured to the United States, by any treaty made with a foreign nation, or by a cession from any state to the United States, which lands had not been previously sold, ceded or leased by the United States, or the claim to which lands had not been previously recognized and confirmed by the United States; and who at the time of passing this act does or do actually inhabit and reside on such lands, may at any time prior to the first day of January next, apply to the proper register or recorder, as the case may be, of the land-office established for the disposal, registering, or recording of such lands, or to such person or persons as may be such registers or recorders respectively, be appointed for the purpose of receiving such applications, stating the tract or tracts of land thus occupied, settled, and inhabited by such applicant or applicants, and requesting permission to continue thereon....

Sec. 4. *And be it further enacted,* That it shall be lawful after the first day of January next, for the proper marshal, or officer acting as marshal, under such instructions as may for that purpose be given by the President of the United States, to remove from the lands aforesaid, any and every person or persons, who shall be found on the same, and who shall not have obtained permission to remain thereon as aforesaid....

Attorney General's Advisory Opinion*

Sir:

Previous to my receiving your note of the 22d instant, Mr. Madison had sent me a lengthy statement of facts relative to the Batture in front of the suburb St. Mary, New Orleans, or alluvial lands to which you refer. On this statement Messrs. Derbigny and Lisley [Moreau Lisletl], French lawyers of reputation, and Mr. Gurley, Attorney General of the New Orleans Territory, have, I understand, given decided opinions in favor of the title of the United States to the Batture. Upon reflection, I concur

*Source: *American State Papers, Public Lands,* vol. 2, p. 12.

with them. The statement I must presume to be correct, as it has been officially furnished.

Under the first section of the act of the 3d of March, A.D. 1807, I am of opinion that military force may be employed by the President to remove from these lands any person who may have taken possession of them since the passage of the law. This, I think, appears to have been the fact in the present case, from the letter of Mr. Van Pradellers, of the 11th ultimo, which I return you. At first I entertained doubts on this point, but further inquiry removed them. These observations contain the requisite answers to the two questions proposed, viz:

1.   Have not the United States a claim to these lands?
2.   If they have may not military possession be taken?

Yours very respectfully and sincerely,
C. A. Rodney

Order to the U.S. Marshal in New Orleans*

Sir:

In pursuance of the provisions of the act of Congress, 'to prevent settlements on lands ceded to the United States, until authorized by law,' I am directed by the president, to instruct you to remove immediately from the land known and called by the name of the Batture, in front of the suburb St. Mary, of the city of New Orleans, which was ceded to the United States by the treaty with France, and the settlement of which has not been authorized by any law of the United States, all persons who shall be found on the same, and who shall have taken possession or settled thereon, since the 3d day of March, in the year 1807. Should any aid be necessary you will call for the assistance of the good citizens of the district, as the *posse comitatus,* or the civil power of the territory. I have the honor to be, very respectfully, Sir, your obedient servant,

James Madison

---

*U.S. Department of State, November 30, 1807. The text of the order appears in *Livingston v. D'Orgenoy,* 11 U.S. (7 Cranch) 577 (1813), at p. 578.

Presidential Message to Congress*

To the Senate and House of Representatives of the United States:

In the city of New Orleans, and adjacent to it, are sundry parcels of ground, some of them with buildings and other improvements on them, which it is my duty to present to the attention of the Legislature. The title to these grounds appears to have been retained in the former sovereigns of the province of Louisiana as public fiduciaries, and for the purposes of the province. Some of them were used for the residence of the Governor, for public offices, hospitals, barracks, magazines, fortifications, levees, &c.; others for the town-house, schools, markets, landings, and other purposes of the city of New Orleans. Some were held by religious corporations or persons; others seem to have been reserved for future disposition.

To these must be added a parcel called the Batture, which requires more particular description. It is understood to have been a shoal, or elevation of the bottom of the river adjacent to the bank of the suburbs of Ste. Marie, produced by the successive depositions of mud during the annual inundations of the river, and covered with water only during those inundations. At all other seasons it has been used by the city immemorially to furnish earth for raising their streets and court-yards, for mortar, and other necessary purposes, and as a landing, or quay, for unloading firewood, lumber, and other articles brought by water. This having lately been claimed by a private individual, the city opposed the claim on a supposed legal title in itself: but it has been adjudged that the legal title was not in the city. It is, however, alleged that that title, originally in the former sovereigns, was never parted with by them, but was retained by them for the uses of the city and province, and, consequently, has now passed over to the United States. Until this question can be decided under legislative authority, measures have been taken according to law to prevent any change in the state of things, and to keep the grounds clear of intruders. The settlement of this title . . . [is] now submitted to the determination of the legislature. . . .

March 7, 1808   Th. Jefferson

---

*Source: *American State Papers, Public Lands,* vol. 2, pp. 15–16.

Resolutions of the Territorial Legislature*

Land in the City of New Orleans, Called the Batture. Communicated to the House of Representatives, March 1, 1810.

Whereas the right of property to the Batture in front of the suburb St. Mary, of New Orleans, is about to be made a question before the honorable the Congress of the United States, and that, on a subject so interesting to the inhabitants of the Territory of Orleans, it is proper that the Legislative Council and House of Representatives should express their sentiments, and more especially that the same may serve as instructions to the delegate from this Territory to the Congress of the United States—

Therefore resolved by the Legislative Council and House of Representatives of the Territory of Orleans, That in their opinion, "the Batture in front to the suburb St. Mary is a shoal or elevation of the bottom of the Mississippi, produced by the successive deposite of mud during the annual rise of the river."

Resolved, That the Batture in front of the suburb St. Mary, being covered with water, generally, from five to six months in each year, and, during that time immemorially used as a great highway, can only be considered a part of the bed of the Mississippi.

Resolved, That the Batture in front of the suburb St. Mary, when not covered by the Mississippi, which is generally from five to six months in each year, having been used "by the city of New Orleans immemorially to furnish earth for raising their streets and court-yard, for mortar, and other necessary purposes, and as a landing, or quay, for unloading firewood, lumber, and other articles brought by water," ought in justice to continue subject to the same uses.

Resolved, further, as the opinion of the Legislative Council and House of Representatives, That the embanking of Batture, in front of the suburb St. Mary, would tend to change the channel of the Mississippi in front of New Orleans, and prove of lasting injury to that port, and that the possession of the said Batture by an individual would subject the citizens of New Orleans, and all the citizens of the United States trading to New Orleans, to the payment of tribute, for a use which the laws of nature, and immemorial custom, and the sanction of the former Spanish Government of Louisiana, secured to them.

*Source: *American State Papers, Public Lands,* vol. 2, p. 102.

Resolved, That these resolutions be signed by the President of the Legislative Council and the Speaker of the House of Representatives, and be by them transmitted to Julian Poydras, Esq. the delegate from the Territory of Orleans to the Congress of the United States.

> Thomas Urquhart
> *Speaker of the House of Representatives.*
> J.D. Degoutin Bellechasse
> *President of the Legislative Council.*

Livingston to Members of Congress*

Sir,

The peculiarity of my situation will justify me in renewing to you individually, the appeal which has repeatedly been made to the honorable body of which you are a member. Without entering into any other circumstances of my case, this much is without dispute,—that without trial or any judicial process, I have, by military force, been driven from the possession of a real estate, of which I was the bona fide purchaser, for a valuable consideration, for a person in possession, and under a title recognised to be good, by the sentence of a competent tribunal, judging in the last resort,—that I am an American citizen and have never done any thing to forefeit the rights to which that quality entitles me; and that the United States being in possession, I have no remedy at law.

Whether the law of 1807, authorises the proceedings against me or not or whatever were the motive of those proceedings, my case is equally one of primary public concern, and is that of every individual in the community, for no one has any *legal* security which I had not. If the law authorises such proceedings, it is unconstitutional; if it do not authorise them, the misconstruction ought to be remedied. I might therefore, Sir, without presumption, *claim* that interference, as a matter of the highest public duty, which in my present position, I am content to *solicit* as a private favor. Deprived of a fortune that would place me in a state of independence, I am, by the act of the government, reduced to poverty,

* Circular letter of Edward Livingston to Members of Congress, June 23, 1809. Miscellaneous Papers, Courtesy of New-York Historical Society.

and exposed to the pursuits of creditors whose patience will, I fear, be exhausted by further delay; twice obliged to leave my profession and place of abode, my means are exhausted, and my business lost. Under these circumstances, Sir, I am persuaded that you will not suffer the trifling inconvenience of a few hours delay, to balance the utter ruin of a fellow citizen who cannot trace misfortune to any imprudence of his own, and who only asks that fair trial which the constitution, you have sworn to defend, secures indiscriminately to all.

Jefferson to William Branch Giles*

Dear Sir,
You have heard of the suit brought by E. Livingston against me on the subject of the Batture. This has rendered it necessary for me to make a statement of the facts for the use of Counsel and the justification which they offer being derived from certain systems of foreign law, in force at N. Orleans, which I have had more time to enquire into than they, I have been led to go into a full investigation of the law and fact of the case. This I now inclose to you with the following view. I am apprehensive that L's assiduities & intrigues may induce Congress to some vote referring his claim to judges or Commissioners. The countenance of such a vote would impress a jury sensibly, and unfavorably and Congress may leave it so with the more propriety inasmuch as L. himself has transferred it from before them to another tribunal. I have thought that I might rely on your justice as well as your friendship to attend to this case in the Senate so far as to prevent his obtaining there any vote injurious to a fair trial. And to satisfy your conscience that this will do him no injustice, I ask your perusal of the inclosed.† I am sensible it is of a revolting length; but the variety and novelty of the points it brings forward will not be unentertaining to you as a lawyer. When you shall have read it be so good as to send it by post to Mr. Eppes, for which purpose I enclose a franked cover. I have requested of him to bestow in the H. of R. the same intention I ask of you in the Senate; and from both I request that no communication of the logic of my defence may be made to any body,

*Jefferson to Giles, November 12, 1810, Jefferson Papers, Library of Congress, Washington, D.C.
† Jefferson enclosed a copy of the brief he had prepared as an aid to counsel.

unless indeed any attempts in Congress might render it necessary to use them there. You are sensible what advantage a knowledge of them would give my adversary. Were this case before an impartial court, it would never give me a moment's concern. But I would never have brought it in such a court. The deep-seated enmity of one judge, & utter nullity of the other, with the precedents of Burr's case, lessen the confidence which the justice of my cause would otherwise give me. Should the Federalists from Livingston's example undertake to harass and run me down, with prosecutions before federal judges, I see neither rest nor safety before me. Wishing you the pleasure of a smooth session, I salute you with all affection.

Jefferson to Madison*

Dear Sir,

I enclose you the extract of a letter from Governor Tyler which will explain itself, and I do it on the same principle on which I have sometimes done the same thing before, that whenever you are called on to select [judicial appointees], you may have under consideration all those who may properly be thought of and the grounds of their pretensions. From what I can learn Griffin cannot stand it long, and really the state has suffered long enough by having such a cypher in so important an office, and infinitely the more from the want of any counterpoint to the rancorous hatred which Marshall bears to the government of his country, and from the cunning and sophistry within which he is able to enshroud himself. It will be difficult to find a character of firmness enough to preserve his independence on the same bench with Marshall. Tyler, I am certain, would do it. He is an able and well read lawyer, about 59 years of age: He was popular as a judge, and is remarkably so as a governor, for his incorruptible integrity, which no circumstances have ever been able to turn from its course. Indeed I think there is scarcely a person in the state so solidly popular, or who would be so much approved for that place. A milk and water character in that office would be seen as a calamity. Tyler having been the former state judge of that court too, and removed to make way for so wretched a fool as Griffin, has a kind of right of reclamation, with the advantage of

* Jefferson to Madison, May 25, 1810, in *The Writings of Thomas Jefferson*, P. L. Ford (ed.), 10 vols. (New York, 1892–1899), vol. 9, p. 276.

repeated elections by the legislature, as admiralty judge, circuit judge, and Governor. But of all these things you will judge fairly between him and his competitors. You have seen in the papers that Livingston has served a writ on me, stating damages at 100,000.D. The ground is not yet explained, but it is understood to be the batture. I have engaged Wirt, Hay, & Wickham as counsel. I shall soon look into my papers to make a state of the case to enable them to plead: and as much of our proceedings was never committed to writing, and my memory cannot be trusted, it is probably I shall have to appeal to that of my associates in the proceedings. I believe that what I did was in harmony with the opinion of all the members of the administration, verbally expressed altho' not in writing. . . .

. . . In speaking of Livingston's suit, I omitted to observe that it is little doubted that his knowledge of Marshall's character has induced him to bring this action. His [i.e., Marshall's] twistifications in the case of Marbury, in that of Burr, and the late Yazoo case show how dexterously he can reconcile law to his personal biasses: and nobody seems to doubt that he is prepared to decide that Livingston's right to the batture is unquestionable, and that I am bound to pay for it with my private fortune. . . .

*Jefferson to Judge John Tyler**

Dear Sir,

Your friendly letter of the 12th has been duly received. Although I have laid it down as a law to myself, never to embarrass the President with my solicitation, and have not till now broken through it, yet I have made a part of your letter the subject of one to him, and have done it with all my heart, and in the full belief that I serve him and the public in urging [your] appointment. We have long enough suffered under the base prostitution of law to party passions in one judge, and the imbecility of another. In the hands of one the law is nothing more than an ambiguous text, to be explained by his sophistry into any meaning which may subserve his personal malice. Nor can any milk-and-water associate maintain his own dependence, and by a firm pursuance of what the law really is, extend its protection to the citizens or the public. I believe you will do it, and where you cannot induce your colleague to do

---

*Jefferson to Tyler, May 26, 1810, in *Writings of Jefferson,* vol. 9, p. 276n.

what is right, you will be firm enough to hinder him from doing what is wrong, and by opposing sense to sophistry, leave the juries free to follow their own judgment....

*Jefferson to George Hay** ══════════════

Dear Sir,

Your favor of July 20 was received on the 24th....

With respect to pleas, I think, if the government should take an interest in the case, I should omit none which may defeat the action in any way. The plea to the jurisdiction therefore, if it can be maintained, should be put in, and especially as it is recommended by the Atty. Genl. The plea that he is a citizen of no state, if a good one, might be tried also, but I think you said, that my oath would be requisite to the fact. That sanction I cannot give, because I know nothing of the fact. If the action should be got rid of in any of these ways, I should immediately lay the case before the public, either directly, or by addressing the justification to Congress.... My defence would not require a single witness. That I did it as the servant of the public, denying corruption, malice or any other criminal motive which could subject me by law. The printed & written information we received was sufficient to justify the interposition of the Executive, who cannot wait for jury findings before he acts. The course, therefore, which the trial is to take is merely to support the right of the public to the batture, in which N.O. is most vitally interested. It is interesting to us to use all the delay possible for reasons before explained in conversation. After you shall have satisfied yourself, by a perusal of the inclosed, as to the pleas to be used, be so good as to re-inclose it to me, that I may forward it to Mr. Tazewell.... I must communicate the same paper to some friends in both houses of Congress. In their present uninformed state, they might by the solicitations of Livingston be led to take some erroneous steps, which might in the eye of a jury amount to an opinion against us; and might encourage the partialities of the judge. I wish it were possible to force it into our state court. The federal condition of all those of the general government leaves me without confidence in a fair decision by any of them.

*Jefferson to Hay, August 1, 1810, Jefferson Papers, Library of Congress, Washington, D.C.

Jefferson to Albert Gallatin*

What the issue of the case ought to be, no unbiased man can doubt. What it will be, no one can tell. The judge's [i.e., Marshall's] inveteracy is profound, and his mind of that gloomy malignity which will never let him forego the opportunity of satiating it on a victim. His decisions, his instructions to a jury, his allowances and disallowances and garbling of evidence, must all be the subjects of appeal. I consider that as my only chance of saving my fortune from entire wreck. And to whom is my appeal? From the judge in Burr's case to himself and his associate judges in the case of Marbury v. Madison. Not exactly, however, I observe old Cushing is dead. At length, then, we have a chance of getting a Republican majority in the Supreme judiciary. For ten years has that branch braved the spirit and will of the nation, after the nation has manifested its will by a complete reform in every branch depending on them. The event is a fortunate one, and so timed as to be a Godsend to me. I am sure its importance to the nation will be felt, and the occasion employed to complete the great operation they have so long been executing, by the appointment of a decided Republican, with nothing equivocal about him. But who will it be?

Jefferson to Madison†

Dear Sir,

... Another circumstance of congratulation is the death of Cushing. The nation ten years ago declared its will for a change in the principles of the administration of their affairs. They then changed the two branches depending on their will, and have steadily maintained the reformation in those branches. The third, not dependent of them, has so long bid defiance to their will, erecting themselves into a political body, to correct what they deem the errors of the nation. The death of Cushing gives an opportunity of closing the reformation by a successor of unquestionable republican principles. Our friend Lincoln has of course presented himself to your recollection. I know you think lightly of him as a lawyer; and I do not consider him a correct common lawyer, yet as much so as any one which ever came, or ever can come from one of the Eastern

* Jefferson to Gallatin, September 27, 1810, in *Writings of Jefferson*, vol. 9, p. 283n.
† Jefferson to Madison, October 15, 1810, in *Writings of Jefferson*, vol. 9, pp. 282–283.

states. Their system of jurisprudence made up from the Jewish law, a little dash of common law, & a great mass of original notions of their own, is a thing sui generis, and one educated in that system can never so far eradicate early impressions as to imbibe thoroughly the principles of another system. It is so in the case of other systems of which Ld. Mansfield is a splendid example. Lincoln's firm republicanism, and known integrity, will give compleat confidence to the public in the long desired reformation of their judiciary. Were he out of the way, I should think Granger prominent for the place. His abilities are great, I have entire confidence in his integrity , tho' I am sensible that J.R. [John Randolph] has been able to lessen the confidence of many in him. But that I believe he would soon reconcile to him, if placed in a situation to show himself to the public, as he is, and not as any enemy has represented him. As the choice must be of a New Englander, to exercise the functions for New England men, I confess to know of none but these two characters. Morton is really a republican, but inferior to both the others in every point of view. Blake calls himself republican, but never was one at Heart. His treachery to us under the embargo should put him by forever. Story & Bacon are exactly the men who deserted us on that measure & carried off the majority. The former unquestionably a tory, & both are too young. I say nothing of professing federalists.... I have said this much because I know you must wish to learn the sentiments of others, to hear all, and then do what on the whole you perceive to be best....

Livingston v. Jefferson*

This was an action of trespass, brought in the circuit court of the United States, for the district of Virginia, by Edward Livingston, a citizen of the state of New York, against Thomas Jefferson, a citizen of the state of Virginia, and late president of the United States, for a trespass alleged to have been committed by the defendant whilst he was president, in removing him from the batture, in the city of New-Orleans, in the then territory of Orleans, now the state of Louisiana. The suit was commenced in 1810, after the expiration of Mr. Jefferson's last term in office.

* 15 Fed. Cases 660 (Cir.Ct.Dist. Va. 1811)

TYLER, DISTRICT JUDGE

... By the common law, which was adopted by an act of convention of this state, so far as it applied to our constitution, then formed, this point has been settled uninterruptedly for centuries past, and recognized by uniform opinion and decisions, both in England and America....

It is enough to say that ... the action for trespass [is] local, and is so held to this day....

[W]here title of land is in question, the action must be local....

Upon the ground taken, so far then, the action cannot be maintained in this court.... But there is no failure of justice; there is a court of competent power to try the cause, if an actual trespass has been committed; and there ought the suit to have been brought against the real trespasser.... [I] therefore must conclude by giving my decided opinion in favor of the plea to the jurisdiction. The cause must therefore go out of court.

MARSHALL, CIRCUIT JUSTICE

The sole question now to be decided is this—Can this court take cognizance of a trespass committed on lands lying within the United States, and without the district of Virginia, in a case where the trespasser is a resident of, and is found within the district? I concur with my brother judge in the opinion that it cannot. I regret that the inconvenience to which delay might expose at least one of the parties, together with the situation of the court, prevent me from bestowing on this question that deliberate consideration which the very able discussion it has received from the bar would seem to require—but I have purposely avoided any investigation of the subject previous to the argument, and must now be content with a brief statement of the opinion I have formed, and a sketch of the course of reasoning which has led to it. The doctrine of actions local and transitory has been traced up to its origin in the common law— and, as has been truly stated on both sides, it appears that originally all actions were local. That is, that according to the principles of the common law, every fact must be tried by a jury of the vicinage. The plain consequence of this principle is, that those courts only could take jurisdiction of a case, who were capable of directing such a jury as must try the material facts on which their judgment would depend....

According to the common law of England then, the distinction taken by the defendant's counsel, between actions local and transitory, is the true distinction, and an action of [trespass] is a local action. This common law has been adopted by the legislature of Virginia. Had it not been adopted, I should have thought it in force. When our ancestors migrated to America, they brought with them the common law of their native country, so far as it was applicable to their new situation; and I do not conceive that the Revolution would, in any degree, have changed the relations of man to man, or the law which regulated those relations. In breaking our political connection with the parent state, we did not break our connection with each other. . . .

The law is in favor of the defendant. . . .

Bibliographic Essay

This brief essay highlights works in the field of legal history that deserve special notice. With few exceptions, the books included are relatively recent. Their contents inform the body of the text of this book even though not all of them appear in the footnote references.

The single most influential book published in the last decade is Morton J. Horwitz, *The Transformation of American Law: 1780–1860* (Cambridge, Mass., 1977), the first of a projected two-volume work that will, when completed, tell the story of American legal development from the Revolution to the twentieth century with exceptional sophistication. Unlike many other works in the history of ideas, Horwitz grounds the legal ideas he analyzes in the changing social and economic conditions of antebellum America. William E. Nelson, *Americanization of the Common Law: The Impact of Legal Change on Massachusetts Society, 1760–1830* (Cambridge, Mass., 1975), is narrower in scope in that it deals with one state. It is also highly technical in its analysis. However, the book is methodologically unique, in that Nelson based his findings on manuscript court records and did not confine his research to reported appellate decisions. While Horwitz and Nelson differ in their interpretive approaches, both works owe much to the pioneering scholarship of James Willard Hurst, whose numerous monographs have profoundly affected modern historians of American law. Hurst's best-known volume is *Law and the Conditions of Freedom in the Nineteenth-Century United States* (Madison, Wis., 1956). Lawrence M. Friedman, *A History of American Law* (New York, 1973), an extraordinarily learned effort to put together a multitude of subjects and sources, encompasses the history of American law from colonial times to the present, but it is strongest on nineteenth-century developments. These volumes supersede Roscoe Pound, *The Formative Era of American Law* (Boston, 1938), which is nevertheless still an interesting and provocative attempt to synthesize antebellum legal history by one of the most influential thinkers to emerge from the Progressive era.

Another overview that has the merit of high readability based on wide-ranging scholarship is Bernard Schwartz, *The Law in America: A History* (New York, 1974). Finally, Grant Gilmore's *The Ages of American Law* (New Haven, Conn., 1977) presents the major themes of American legal history in a short but provocative volume.

Two recent anthologies contain useful materials for selective reading and study: *Essays in Nineteenth-Century American Legal History* (Westport, Conn., 1976), edited by Wythe Holt, reproduces the most important articles to have appeared recently in law reviews and other scholarly journals; and Stephen B. Presser and Jamil S. Zainaldin, *Law and American History: Cases and Materials* (St. Paul, Minn., 1980), which is a casebook volume with interesting primary materials. Perry Miller's annotated collection of documents, *The Legal Mind in America: From Independence to the Civil War* (New York, 1962), is still a valuable supplementary source on jurisprudential thought.

Books on specialized subjects that have been touched on in the text are Maxwell Bloomfield, *American Lawyers in a Changing Society, 1776–1876* (Cambridge, Mass., 1976), on lawyers and the legal profession; Richard Ellis, *The Jeffersonian Crisis: Courts and Politics in the Young Republic* (New York, 1971), on the interface between law and politics; Leonard W. Levy, *The Law of the Commonwealth and Chief Justice Shaw* (Cambridge, Mass., 1957), on the impact of a major state judge on the development of public and private law; Robert A. Rutland, *The Birth of the Bill of Rights* (Chapel Hill, N.C., 1955), the best history of the first ten amendments to the Constitution; and Mark DeWolfe Howe, *The Garden and the Wilderness: Religion and Government in American Constitutional History* (Chicago, 1965), a most penetrating analysis of this complex issue.

Many manuscript sources for legal history have been edited and published in recent years. One of the best is L. Kinvin Wroth and Hiller B. Zobel (eds.), *Legal Papers of John Adams*, 3 vols. (Cambridge, Mass., 1965).

For further background on the Batture controversy, consult the following works, each of which presents a somewhat different viewpoint: Dumas Malone, *Jefferson and His Time,* 6 vols. (Boston, 1948–1981), vol. 6: *The Sage of Monticello,* chap. 5, which supports Jefferson's Batture policy; Edward Dumbauld, *Thomas Jefferson and the Law* (Norman, Okla., 1978), chap. 3, which is strong on legal aspects of the case; and George Dargo, *Jefferson's Louisiana: Politics and the Clash of Legal Traditions* (Cambridge, Mass., 1975), chap. 4, which is critical of Jefferson on this issue.

The epigraph to this book is a quotation from the father of American legal history, and this bibliography would not be complete without the inclusion of his great book, which in 1981 celebrated its centennial: Oliver Wendell Holmes, Jr., *The Common Law* (1881), one of the great American books on the history and development of the law.

Index

Action on the case, definition of, 98n
ADAMS, JOHN QUINCY, 51, 113
ADAMS, WILLI PAUL, 10n, 12n
Administrative law, 8
Adverse possession, definition of, 110n
Agency law, 8
Agriculture, 1, 2
Ahlstrom, Sidney E., 19n
Alexander, James, 50–51
American Revolution, 1, 2
  and fear of political excess, 17, 18
  impact of, on law, 7–9
  as lawyer's revolution, 7
Angell, Joseph K., 34n
Antifederalists, 15
Appointed officials, versus elected officials, and libel, 24, 90
Apprentice law clerks, 49–51
Articles of Confederation (1781), 16, 71–72

Bailyn, B., 32n
Baldwin, Henry, 51
Bar, joinder of bench and, 57
Bartlett, Ichabod, 44
Batture Controversy, 107–136
Beard, Charles A., 12n
Bench, joinder of bar and, 57
Bentham, Jeremy, 27n
Berger, Raoul, 15n
Berman, Harold J., 29n
Bickel, Alexander, 98n

About the Author

GEORGE DARGO did his undergraduate work at Columbia College and completed his doctorate in History in the Graduate Faculties, Columbia University, in 1970. During the academic year 1976–1977 Mr. Dargo attended the Harvard Law School as a Liberal Arts Fellow in Law and History and received study grants from the American Council of Learned Societies and the Social Science Research Council. He has taught United States History and American Legal History at various academic institutions including the City University of New York, the University of Massachusetts, and Holy Cross College in Worcester, Massachusetts. Following his graduation in 1981 from the Northeastern University Law School, Mr. Dargo served as a Law Clerk for the Honorable Rya W. Zobel in the United States District Court in Boston. He is a member of the Massachusetts Bar and currently practices law in Boston, Massachusetts where he is associated with the law firm of Widett, Slater & Goldman, P.C. Mr. Dargo's publications include two previous books, *Roots of the Republic: A New Perspective on Early American Constitutionalism* (1974) and *Jefferson's Louisiana: Politics and the Clash of Legal Traditions* (1975).

A Note on the Type

The text of this book was set in a computer version of Times Roman, designed by Stanley Morison for *The Times* (London) and first introduced by that newspaper in 1932.

Among typographers and designers of the twentieth century, Stanley Morison has been a strong forming influence as typographical adviser to the English Monotype Corporation, as a director of two distinguished English publishing houses, and as a writer of sensibility, erudition, and keen practical sense.

Typography by Barbara Sturman. Cover design by Maria Epes. Composition by Delmas Typesetting, Ann Arbor, Michigan. Printed and bound by Banta Company, Menasha, Wisconsin.

BORZOI BOOKS
IN LAW AND AMERICAN SOCIETY

Law and American History

EARLY AMERICAN LAW AND SOCIETY
Stephen Botein, *Michigan State University*

This volume consists of an essay dealing with the nature of law and early American socioeconomic development from the first settlements to 1776. The author shows how many legal traditions sprang both from English experience and from the influence of the New World. He explores the development of transatlantic legal structures in order to show how they helped rationalize intercolonial affairs. Mr. Botein also emphasizes the relationship between law and religion. The volume includes a pertinent group of documents for classroom discussion, and a bibliographic essay.

LAW IN THE NEW REPUBLIC: *Private Law and the Public Estate*
George Dargo, *Brookline, Massachusetts*

Though the American Revolution had an immediate and abiding impact on American public law (e.g., the formation of the federal and state constitutions), its effect on private law (e.g., the law of contracts, tort law) was less direct but of equal importance. Through essay and documents, Mr. Dargo examines post-Revolutionary public and private reform impulses and finds a shifting emphasis from public to private law which he terms "privatization." To further illustrate the tension between public and private law, the author develops a case study (the Batture land controversy in New Orleans) in early nineteenth century legal, economic, and political history. The volume includes a wide selection of documents and a bibliographic essay.

LAW IN ANTEBELLUM SOCIETY: *Legal Change and Economic Expansion*
Jamil Zainaldin, *Washington, D.C.*

This book examines legal change and economic expansion in the first half of the nineteenth century, integrating major themes in the development of law with key historical themes. Through a series of topical essays and the use of primary source materials, it describes how political, social, and economic interests and values influence law making. The book's focus is on legislation and the common law.

LAW AND THE NATION, 1865–1912
Jonathan Lurie, *Rutgers University*

Using the Fourteenth Amendment as the starting point for his essay, Mr. Lurie examines the ramifications of this landmark constitutional provision on the economic and social development of America in the years following the Civil War. He also explores important late nineteenth-century developments in legal education, and concludes his narrative with some insights on law and social change in the first decade of the twentieth century. The volume is highlighted by a documents section containing statutes, judicial opinions, and legal briefs, with appropriate questions for classroom discussion. Mr. Lurie's bibliographic essay provides information to stimulate further investigation of this period.

ORDERED LIBERTY: *Legal Reform in the Twentieth Century*
Gerald L. Fetner, *University of Chicago*

In an interpretive essay, the author examines the relationship between several major twentieth-century reform movements (e.g., Progressivism, New Deal, and the Great Society) and the law. He shows how policy makers turned increasingly to the legal community for assistance in accommodating economic and social conflict, and how the legal profession responded by formulating statutes, administrative agencies, and private arrangements. Mr. Fetner also discusses how the organization and character of the legal profession were affected by these social changes. Excerpts from relevant documents illustrate issues discussed in the essay. A bibliographic essay is included.

Law and Philosophy

DISCRIMINATION AND REVERSE DISCRIMINATION
Kent Greenawalt, *Columbia Law School*

Using discrimination and reverse discrimination as a model, Mr. Greenawalt examines the relationship between law and ethics. He finds that the proper role of law cannot be limited to grand theory concerning individual liberty and social restraint, but must address what law can effectively discover and accomplish. Such concepts as distributive and compensatory justice and utility are examined in the context of preferential treatment for blacks and other minorities. The analysis draws heavily on the Supreme Court's Bakke decision. The essay is followed by related documents, primarily judicial opinions, with notes and questions, and a bibliography.

THE LEGAL ENFORCEMENT OF MORALITY
Thomas Grey, *Stanford Law School*

This book deals with the traditional issue of whether morality can be legislated and enforced. It consists of an introductory essay and legal texts on three issues: the enforcement of sexual morality, the treatment of human remains, and the duties of potential rescuers. The author shows how philosophical problems differ from classroom hypotheticals when they are confronted in a legal setting. He illustrates this point using material from statutes, regulations, judicial opinions, and law review commentaries. Mr. Grey reviews the celebrated Hart-Devlin debate over the legitimacy of prohibiting homosexual acts. He places the challenging problem of how to treat dead bodies, arising out of developments in the technology of organ transplantation, in the context of the debate over morals enforcement, and discusses the Good Samaritan as an issue concerning the propriety of the legal enforcement of moral duties.

LEGAL REASONING
Martin Golding, *Duke University*

This volume is a blend of text and readings. The author explores the many sides to legal reasoning—as a study in judicial psychology and, in a more narrow sense, as an inquiry into the "logic" of judicial decision making. He shows how judges justify their rulings, and gives examples of the kinds of arguments they use. He challenges the notion that judicial reasoning is rationalization; instead, he argues that judges are guided by a deep concern for consistency and by a strong need to have their decisions stand as a measure for the future conduct of individuals. *(Forthcoming in 1984)*

Law and American Literature

LAW AND AMERICAN LITERATURE
A one-volume collection of the following three essays:

Law as Form and Theme in American Letters
Carl S. Smith, *Northwestern University*

The author explores the interrelationships between law aned literature generally and between American law and American literature in particular. He explores first the literary qualities of legal writing and then the attitudes of major American writers toward the law. Throughout, he studies the links between the legal and literary imaginations. He finds that legal writing has many literary qualities that are essential to its function, and he points out that American writers have long been wary of the power of the law and its special language, speaking out as a compensating voice for the ideal of justice.

Innocent Criminal or Criminal Innocence: The Trial in American Fiction
John McWilliams, *Middlebury College*

Mr. McWilliams explores how law functions as a standard for conduct in a number of major works of American literature, including Cooper's *The Pioneers,* Melville's *Billy Budd,* Dreiser's *An American Tragedy,* and Wright's *Native Son.* Each of these books ends in a criminal trial, in which the reader is asked to choose between his emotional sympathy for the victim and his rational understanding of society's need for criminal sanctions. The author compares these books with James Gould Cozzens' *The Just and the Unjust,* a study of a small town legal system, in which the people's sense of justice contravenes traditional authority.

Law and Lawyers in American Popular Culture
Maxwell Bloomfield, *Catholic University of America*

Melding law, literature, and the American historical experience into a single essay, Mr. Bloomfield discusses popular images of the lawyer. The author shows how contemporary values and attitudes toward the law are reflected in fiction. He concentrates on two historical periods: antebellum America and the Progressive era. He examines fictional works which were not always literary classics, but which exposed particular legal mores. An example of such a book is Winston Churchill's *A Far Country* (1915), a story of a successful corporation lawyer who abandons his practice to dedicate his life to what he believes are more socially desirable objectives.